BRAQUE

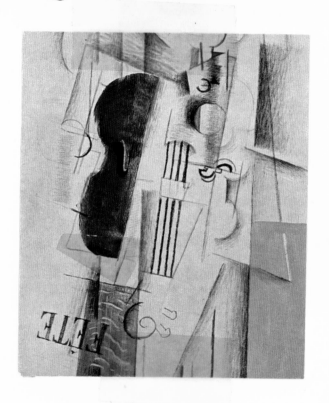

Title page:
Violin (detail), 1913. Papier collé.
Courtesy Philadelphia Museum of Art,
Louise and Walter Arensberg Collection.

✳

© by Editions d'Art Albert Skira, 1961.
Library of Congress Catalog Card Number: 61-10170.
All reproduction rights reserved by Association pour la Diffusion
des Arts Graphiques et Plastiques, A.D.A.G.P., Paris.

✳

Distributed in the United States by
THE WORLD PUBLISHING COMPANY
2231 West 110th Street - Cleveland 2, Ohio.

CHRONOLOGICAL SURVEY

1882 Born at Argenteuil-sur-Seine, near Paris, on May 13, son of Charles Braque and Augustine Johanet. His father and grandfather owned and managed a house-painting business in the Rue de l'Hôtel-Dieu.

1881 Birth of Pablo Picasso, October 25.

1890 The Braque family moves to Le Havre.

1893 Braque enters the Lycée at Le Havre.

1897 Attends evening classes at the local Ecole des Beaux-Arts (Professor Courchet), where Raoul Dufy and Othon Friesz, both natives of Le Havre, had studied before him. Takes music lessons from one of the Dufy brothers.

1899 Leaves school and is apprenticed to a house-painter named Roney.

1900 Goes to Paris to complete his apprenticeship under M. Laberthe, a friend and former employee of his father. Lives in Montmartre, Rue des Trois-Frères. Studies drawing and painting in evening classes at the Cours Municipal des Batignolles (Professor Quignolot).

1900 Friesz and Dufy at the Ecole des Beaux-Arts, Paris.
Picasso's first visit to Paris.

1901 Called up in October for a year's military service in the 129th Infantry Regiment, stationed near Le Havre.

1901 Death of Toulouse-Lautrec.
Van Gogh retrospective at the Galerie Bernheim-Jeune.

1902 Returns to Montmartre in the fall and takes lodgings in the Rue Lepic. Studies painting at the Académie Humbert, where he meets Marie Laurencin and Francis Picabia. Assiduous visits to the Louvre (Egyptian and archaic Greek sculpture, Poussin and Corot), the Musée du Luxembourg (Caillebotte Bequest), and the Vollard and Durand-Ruel galleries.

1902 Lautrec retrospective at the Indépendants and Durand-Ruel's.

1903 Spends two months in the fall in Léon Bonnat's class at the Ecole des Beaux-Arts, then returns to the Académie Humbert.

1903 Founding of the Salon d'Automne.

1904 Holidays in Brittany and Normandy. On his return to Paris, he decides he has had enough of academic instruction, takes a studio in the Rue d'Orsel and begins painting on his own.

1904 Settling in Paris for good, Picasso takes a studio in the Bateau-Lavoir.

1905 Spends the summer at Honfleur and Le Havre. "View of the Park" (Musée des Beaux-Arts, Le Havre). Becomes friendly with the sculptor Manolo and the critic Maurice Raynal.

1905 Seurat and Van Gogh retrospective at the Indépendants. The Fauves create a sensation at the Salon d'Automne.

1906 Exhibits seven paintings in March at the Salon des Indépendants. Painting trip to Antwerp with Friesz during the summer. Enters the ranks of the Fauves. Moves in October to L'Estaque, near Marseilles.

1906 Death of Cézanne. Juan Gris arrives in Paris. Gauguin retrospective at the Salon d'Automne.

1907 Returns to Paris in February, and in March exhibits six paintings (all sold) at the Indépendants. Meets Matisse, Derain and Vlaminck. Goes in May to La Ciotat, near Toulon, where Friesz soon joins him; they work at L'Estaque in September and return to Paris in October. Braque signs a contract with the dealer D.H. Kahnweiler, who introduces him to Apollinaire. The latter takes him to Picasso's studio in the Bateau-Lavoir where he sees "Les Demoiselles d'Avignon." In December he begins a "Nude" (Cuttoli Collection, Paris).

1907 Cézanne retrospective at the Salon d'Automne.

1908 Spring and summer at L'Estaque where Dufy joins him for a while. First cubist paintings under the influence of Cézanne. In October his pictures are rejected by the jury of the Salon d'Automne; he exhibits them in November in a one-man show at Kahnweiler's gallery (27 items, preface by Apollinaire). Reviewing the exhibition in the Gil Blas (November 14), Louis Vauxcelles speaks of "cubes."

1908 Banquet in Picasso's studio in honor of the Douanier Rousseau.

1909 Exhibits two paintings in March at the Indépendants. Works during the summer at La Roche-Guyon, near Mantes, then with Derain at Carrières-Saint-Denis. In the fall his relations with Picasso ripen into close friendship: Analytical Cubism.

1909 Picasso works in Spain at Horta de San Juan. First performances of Diaghilev's Ballets Russes in Paris.

1910 Takes a studio in the Rue Caulaincourt. Returns to L'Estaque in the summer, while Picasso works at Cadaquès, in Spain, with Derain.

1911 Spends the summer at Céret (French Pyrenees) with Picasso. Hermetic phase of Analytical Cubism. Numbers and letters of the alphabet appear on his canvases. "The Portuguese" (Kunstmuseum, Basel).

1912 Marries Marcelle Lapré. In July he rents a house at Sorgues, near Avignon, where Picasso is staying. In September he produces the first "papier collé."
Synthetic Cubism. Mixes sand with his pigments and paints imitation marble and wood graining.

1912 Gleizes and Metzinger publish "Du Cubisme."

1913 Brief visit in early summer to Céret (where Picasso, Gris and Max Jacob are staying), then goes on to Sorgues.

1913 Armory Show in New York.

1914 The outbreak of war finds him at Sorgues (Derain and Picasso are at Avignon). Mobilized and sent to the front. Twice mentioned in dispatches.

1915 Wounded in the head on May 11 in the fighting at Carency (Artois); trepanned; long convalescence.

1916 Goes to Sorgues in April on sick leave. Discharged as unfit for further service.

1917 His friends throw a banquet in his honor in Paris (January 15) to celebrate his return and recovery. Friendly with Juan Gris and Henri Laurens. "The Musician" (Kunstmuseum, Basel). Léonce Rosenberg becomes his dealer. In December he publishes "Pensées et Réflexions sur la Peinture" in the review Nord-Sud edited by his friend Pierre Reverdy.

1917 In Rome Picasso designs sets and costumes for "Parade."

1918 Mature phase of Synthetic Cubism. Still Lifes on a Table ("Guéridons").

1918 Death of Guillaume Apollinaire.

1919 Exhibits in March at Léonce Rosenberg's gallery, "L'Effort Moderne."

1919 Death of Renoir. Delgrange concerts.

1920 Kahnweiler opens the Galerie Simon and again becomes his dealer. First piece of sculpture: "Standing Nude" (plaster). Woodcuts for the "Piège de Méduse" of Erik Satie.

1922 Moves from Montmartre to Montparnasse (Avenue Reille). Classical period. Begins his "Canephori" and "Mantelpieces." A room devoted to Braque's work at the Salon d'Automne.

1923 Sets for "Les Fâcheux," a Diaghilev ballet with music by Georges Auric.

1924 Exhibits in May at the gallery of his new dealer, Paul Rosenberg. Count Etienne de Beaumont commissions sets from him for the ballet "Salade" (Soirées de Paris).

1924 André Breton publishes the Surrealist Manifesto.

1925 Braque moves into the house built for him by the architect Auguste Perret, at 6 Rue du Douanier, near the Parc Montsouris. Sets for the Diaghilev ballet "Zéphyre et Flore."

1927 Death of Juan Gris.

1928 Change of style. Series of "Guéridons."

1929 Holiday at Dieppe. Begins a series of small seascapes.

1930 Buys and fits up a country house at Varengeville, near Dieppe.

1931 Incised plaster panels with mythological figures. Etchings for Hesiod's "Theogony."

1932 Picasso retrospective at the Galerie Georges Petit, Paris.

1933 First large-scale Braque retrospective in April at the Kunsthalle, Basel.

1934 Exhibition in London at the Reid and Lefèvre Galleries.

1936 Retrospective at the Palais des Beaux-Arts, Brussels. Interiors with figures, decorative still lifes.

1937 Awarded first prize at the Carnegie International, Pittsburgh, for "The Yellow Tablecloth" (Marx Collection, Chicago).

1937 Picasso paints "Guernica."

1939 Paints his first "Studio" (Private Collection, New York). Takes up sculpture at Varengeville.

1939-1940 Braque retrospective held in Chicago, Washington and San Francisco.

1940 Spring at Varengeville. After the German invasion he takes refuge in the Limousin, then in the Pyrenees. Returns to Paris in the fall and remains there throughout the occupation.

1943 Special room devoted to his work at the Salon d'Automne.

1944 Returns to Varengeville in September. Begins the series of "Billiard Tables."

1945 Serious illness: unable to work for several months. Exhibitions in Amsterdam (Stedelijk Museum) and Brussels (Palais des Beaux-Arts).

1946 Color lithographs, pulled by Mourlot. Exhibits with Rouault at the Tate Gallery, London.

1947 First exhibition in June at the gallery of his new dealer, Aimé Maeght, Rue de Téhéran, Paris.

1947 Death of Bonnard and Marquet.

1948 Awarded first prize for painting at the Venice Biennale.

1948-1949 Large-scale Braque retrospective at the Cleveland Museum of Art and the Museum of Modern Art, New York.

1949 Paints the "Terraces" and finishes the first pictures of the "Studio" series. Sets for Molière's "Tartuffe," commissioned by Louis Jouvet.

1952 Exhibition in Tokyo.

1952-1953 Paints ceiling decorations in the Salle Henri II at the Louvre, commissioned by Georges Salles, Director of French Museums.

1953 Retrospective in Bern (Kunsthalle) and Zurich (Kunsthaus).

1953 Death of Dufy.

1953-1954 Designs stained-glass windows for a small church at Varengeville. Decorations for Aimé Maeght's villa at Saint-Paul-de-Vence.

1954 Death of Matisse.

1955 Death of Léger.

1956 End of the "Studio" series. Paintings and lithographs on the "Bird" theme. Important retrospective held in conjunction with the Edinburgh Music Festival and at the Tate Gallery, London.

1958 Exhibits at the Venice Biennale and at the Palazzo Barberini, Rome.

1958 Death of Rouault.

1960 Retrospectives at the Kunsthalle, Basel, and at the Bibliothèque Nationale, Paris (graphic work).

I met Braque under the best auspices, through Nicolas de Staël, at that time still unknown. During one of my first visits to his Paris studio in the Rue du Douanier, Braque was kind enough to show me his jealously guarded Carnets de Dessins; *then he took me into his room where he keeps his dearest possessions: a landscape by his father, a house painter, who taught him the fundamentals of his art, and a still life by Cézanne, his spiritual guide. It represents a bouquet of full-blown flowers surrounded by spacious tracts of unpainted canvas. With a sweep of his hand, Braque silently indicated the immense space separating the flowers from the vase in which they sink their roots. We looked at the picture a long while, then he said: "In Matisse and Manet you get only the flower; in Cézanne you get the flower and the root as well. And what counts is the way he goes from the root to the flower; there a whole life is summed up." A recent remark in his* Cahier *emphasizes this difference: "Some works make you think of the artist, others of the man. I've often heard of Manet's talent, never of Cézanne's."*

Without either seeking or foreseeing the destiny in store for him, Braque has found in painting a supreme fulfillment. For him the evolution of his work has been a way of life. And if in retrospect it is possible to trace the stages, as I have tried to do here, through which his life's work has passed, his inner growth escapes us, though the facts may occasionally shed light on it. Much is to be learned about him from Blaise Cendrars, Guillaume Apollinaire, Carl Einstein, Jean Paulhan, Francis Ponge, Antoine Tudal and René Char; and, most enlightening of all, from the fraternal testimony of Pierre Reverdy entitled Une Aventure Méthodique, *a book that deserves to be better known.*

"In art," says Braque, "there is only one thing worth while, and that is what cannot be explained." But he goes on to add: "You must not ask of the artist more than he can give, nor of the critic more than he can see." Heroic pathfinders through the world of creative art, the painter and the poet reveal true knowledge, true cognition. As he follows in their steps, the critic's role is that of re-cognition.

I take pleasure here in expressing my gratitude to Georges Braque. I dedicate this book to the memory of Nicolas de Staël and Pierre Reverdy.

LANDSCAPE AT LA CIOTAT, 1907. PRIVATE COLLECTION, FRANCE.

FROM IMPRESSIONISM TO FAUVISM

GEORGES BRAQUE was born on May 13, 1882, at Argenteuil, now disfigured by industrial plants and absorbed into the tentacular suburbs of Paris, but at that time a pleasant riverside village outside the city, and a haunt of painters, boating enthusiasts and holiday makers. Monet had lived at Argenteuil from 1872 to 1878 in the palmy days of Impressionism, and the villa on the opposite bank of the Seine that was pointed out to Braque as a child—one of his earliest memories— was the home of Caillebotte, friend and patron of the Impressionists. Natives of Argenteuil, and not of Normandy as often supposed, Braque's father and grandfather owned and managed a house-painting business; in their spare time, for their own pleasure, they painted landscape studies in the open air. Braque still has a view of the Seine, with a bridge and boats, in silver-gray tonalities reminiscent of Corot, painted by his father in the eighties.

In 1890 the family moved to Le Havre and prospered there. After Argenteuil, where Impressionism had reached maturity, the eight-year-old boy now found himself in Normandy, on the Channel coast, the birthplace of Impressionism, that green and sunny country around Honfleur and the Seine estuary beloved of so many painters before him, which was also to cast its spell over Braque. Like Monet, he was uncomfortable on the hard benches of the schoolroom. He preferred sports and the outdoor life, swimming, boating, cycling, hiking; later he even took to boxing. By the time he had grown to manhood he had the physique of an athlete. Though neither moody nor unsociable, he was already reserved and thoughtful, going for long solitary rambles over the countryside and musing by the sea, symbol of infinity. Nothing is more stimulating to a young artist's imagination than the sight of a busy port, and picturesque Le Havre—picturesque no longer, alas!—kept him fascinated, with its breakwater built of stout oak pilings, with its roadsteads and docks winding almost into the heart of the city. By lamplight in the evening he copied the illustrations in the *Gil Blas*, or in the dark streets he detached posters by Lautrec and Steinlen from hoardings. On Sundays he and his father drove into the country in the family buggy and sketched in the open air. At the local museum he discovered canvases by Boudin and Corot. Already a music lover, he learned to play the flute from Gaston Dufy (brother of Raoul), who later gave piano lessons to Jean Dubuffet.

An indifferent pupil at the Lycée, undistinguished even in the drawing class (by no means a child prodigy like Picasso), Braque left school at seventeen to enter his father's business, though he continued to attend evening classes at the local Ecole des Beaux-Arts. In the fall of 1900—at the very time when Picasso, his senior by six months, was paying his first visit to the city—Braque's parents sent him to Paris to finish his apprenticeship under one of their former employees, Laberthe, and to take his diploma as a house painter. By the terms of French law at the time, once he had become a qualified craftsman, his period of obligatory military service was reduced from three years to one year. Besides this immediate benefit and the livelihood it procured him, this early training of his, carried through with such scrupulous thoroughness, was to have far-reaching effects not only on Braque's own art but on the whole evolution of Cubism. Perhaps it also accounts for the domestic orientation of his work, in which landscapes and figures are rare, and which is concerned rather—as befits a highly skilled house decorator—with interiors, with objects, with wall decoration. "Braque," wrote Roger Bissière with great insight in 1920, in the first monograph on the painter, "inherited the trade secrets and formulas which, when all is said and done, are perhaps the essentials of painting, or anyhow its soundest basis." Of Ingres himself we are told that he stopped with his pupils one day in the street and commended to them the example of a house painter, who, as Ingres pointed out, "with the tip of his brush took *just* the amount of paint required and not a drop more." This, the economy and precision of the skilled workman, was instilled into Braque at an early age, and in keeping with the best French tradition his genius lies first of all in his scrupulous craftsmanship, his respect for his tools and materials, his delight in the mysterious powers to which they give form.

During his first year in Paris he lived in Montmartre, Rue des Trois-Frères, and in the evenings attended drawing classes at the Cours Municipal des Batignolles. In October 1901 he was called up and spent a year in the army, stationed near Le Havre. Serving in the same regiment were the picture dealer Jean Dieterle and the collector Albert Henraux; neither had any inkling of Braque's vocation and saw him only as a strapping young fellow with a zest for boxing, who played the accordion and sang and danced better than any of his comrades. Braque had grown up so naturally in an atmosphere of paints and painting that it never occurred to him to adopt any other way of life. "I no more decided to become a painter than I decided to breathe. As far back as I can remember I was never faced with a conscious choice. I think it was Nietzsche who said 'An aim is a servitude,' and it's true. It does a man no good to realize that he's a painter. If I had any aim at all, it was simply to perform each day's task to the best of my ability. In doing so, it turned out that what I produced resembled a picture. I go my way and do the same today, it's as simple as that."

After his discharge from the army he obtained his father's permission to study art in Paris; he was granted a monthly

15

allowance and settled again in Montmartre late in 1902, this time in the Rue Lepic, where Van Gogh had lived fifteen years before. Except for a few months in 1903 in the studio of Bonnat, whose hidebound academicism he found intolerable, Braque spent the next two years studying at the Académie Humbert, in the Boulevard Rochechouart, where a suppler discipline reigned; there he met Marie Laurencin and Francis Picabia. During the summer holidays he painted in Normandy and Brittany. He later destroyed nearly all these early efforts— sensitive and appealing works, of no particular brilliance. Those that survive are chiefly portraits which he gave to the sitters. The *Breton Girl* (Rosensaft Collection, New York), painted in the summer of 1904, is one of them; it shows, along with the influence of Corot, a direct yet discreet approach to the figure (half length, full face, with lowered eyes) and an innate sense of the physical properties of the paints and their resonance. Returning to Paris in 1904 after the summer holidays, he rented a studio of his own in the Rue d'Orsel, across from the Théâtre Montmartre, and feeling that there was nothing more to be gained from the art schools, he decided now to work on independently.

Familiar with the Louvre since boyhood, he had been particularly impressed by Poussin and Corot, by Egyptian and Greek archaic sculpture. He studied the Impressionists at Durand-Ruel's and Vollard's, and in the rooms containing the Caillebotte Bequest at the Musée du Luxembourg. Unattracted by Manet and Degas, his preferences went to Renoir and Monet, a little later to Cézanne and Seurat, who both made a powerful impression on him. At Honfleur, in the early summer of 1905, he painted a *View of the Park* (Musée des Beaux-Arts, Le Havre) with figures seated on a bench, a work still dark and clumsily handled, timidly following in the steps of Monet and Pissarro. Thereafter—though no intermediate pictures survive to mark the stages—Braque evidently made rapid progress, for a few months later he painted a *Ship in Harbor, Le Havre* (Silberman Galleries, New York), soundly constructed and shown in close-up with great technical adroitness. Masts and rigging cut across the composition, forming a harmonious pattern; light glows between sky and water,

SHIP IN HARBOR, LE HAVRE, 1905.
COLLECTION OF E. AND A. SILBERMAN GALLERIES, NEW YORK.

THE PORT OF ANTWERP, 1906.
THE NATIONAL GALLERY OF CANADA, OTTAWA.

while his colors (to which the creamy whites central to his work give both their force and their restraint) are rich and full-bodied as never before.

Braque was moving toward Fauvism, which had just created a sensation at the Salon d'Automne of 1905. This paroxysmal movement was based on the simplification of the painter's

THE PORT OF LA CIOTAT, 1907.
COLLECTION OF THE HON. JOHN HAY WHITNEY, NEW YORK.

means, on the excited handling of pure flat colors, used expressively, not imitatively, as the ideal equivalent of light and the organic principle of the composition. Three main groups, each with a different background, contributed to the rise of Fauvism in France: the ex-students from Gustave Moreau's studio and the Académie Carrière, headed by Matisse and Marquet; a pair of boisterous young men from Chatou, Vlaminck and Derain, who manipulated their color tubes like "dynamite cartridges"; and the late-comers from Le Havre, with impressionist filiations, Dufy (born in 1877), Friesz (born in 1879) and Braque, who followed each other at close intervals through the Lycée and the Ecole des Beaux-Arts of their home town. The three groups

THE LITTLE BAY AT LA CIOTAT, 1907.
SIDNEY JANIS GALLERY, NEW YORK.

were soon welded into one thanks to the prestige and tireless efforts of Matisse, eldest of them all and acknowledged leader of the movement, its lucid theorist and its most complete interpreter. The sight of his work in the fall of 1904 converted Friesz to Fauvism; in the spring of 1905 it won over Dufy. Dazzled by "the miracle of the creative imagination at play in color and design" (Dufy), the two Havrais abandoned impressionist naturalism and, following the lead of Matisse, flung themselves into what Friesz was later to call "colored orchestrations" and "emotional transpositions." At the epoch-making Salon d'Automne of 1905, before the scintillating canvases Matisse and Derain had just brought back from Collioure, it was Braque's turn to experience the decisive revelation. "Matisse and Derain," he acknowledged, "showed me the way." He received his technical initiation from his fellow townsman, Friesz, an unequal creator but a remarkable executant, and like Pissarro, who advised and encouraged him, a gifted and inspiring teacher.

After exhibiting, for the first time, seven landscapes and still lifes at the Salon des Indépendants in March 1906— transitional canvases, all destroyed later—Braque joined Friesz on a painting trip to Antwerp, while Marquet and Dufy went off together to Normandy. Son of a sailor, and a great admirer of Rubens, Friesz was thus doubly attracted by the Baroque charms of the great Flemish port, where he had already worked in 1905. While enjoying the benefit of the elder man's experience, Braque at once asserted his own personality. At Antwerp he painted a dozen canvases which, by his own admission, inaugurated his really creative work. In spite of inevitable hesitations and a certain vacillation between space and surface, light and color, and in spite of his need for realistic supports, the accuracy and felicity of his vision are already apparent, together with his lyrical composure and his power of continual enrichment.

The two friends shared a studio on the Scheldt, with a balcony overlooking the harbor and its colorful traffic, which they evoked together, side by side, Friesz nervously, with brisk and summary accents, Braque with greater assiduity and thoughtful deliberation. In an initial version of great charm (National Gallery of Canada, Ottawa), though still attentive to atmospheric effects, he displays his specific range of serene and limpid colors, gracefully rounds off the long curve of the balustrade (which Friesz schematized), and lingers with ornamental care (reminiscent of Dufy) over the volutes of the grillwork.

Vaporous and mobile, the northern light failed to lend itself to treatment in terms of pure tones of flat color. After stopping over in Paris (September-October 1906), where he tried out his newly acquired technique on one of Sisley's favorite motifs, the *Canal Saint-Martin* (Norbert Schimmel Collection, New York, and Private Collection, Oxford), Braque went down to the South of France and settled at L'Estaque, near Marseilles, one of the sites made famous by Cézanne (and by Renoir), where board and lodging at the Hôtel Maurin were cheap, the climate favorable to winter work, and the bay with its surrounding ridge of mountains rich in superb motifs. He rid himself of the last vestiges of Impressionism, resolutely adopted the style and palette of Fauvism, set the picture surface glowing with the incandescent patchwork of flat colors elaborated by Matisse and Derain, and enlarged on the curvilinear rhythms and decorative arrangements of Gauguin (Samuel A. Berger Collection, New York).

Returning to Paris in February 1907, he entered into direct contact with Matisse, Derain and Vlaminck and exhibited six paintings in March at the Salon des Indépendants, and sold them all, five of them to the critic and dealer Wilhelm Uhde, who had already bought pictures from Picasso and the Douanier Rousseau. Encouraged by these results he went back to the

VIEW FROM THE HÔTEL MISTRAL, L'ESTAQUE, 1907.
COLLECTION OF MR AND MRS WERNER E. JOSTEN, NEW YORK.

Riviera in May, settling this time at La Ciotat, between Marseilles and Toulon. As before at Antwerp and L'Estaque, he painted the port from above, but completely immobilized now in the bright sunlight of the southern summer (John Hay Whitney Collection, New York). Saturated colors alone sufficed to render the full intensity of shimmering light, without atmospheric diffusion. Braque drew his iridescent magic not from pure tones in violent contrast, but from rare and reticent harmonies of mauve, orange, old gold and cyclamen, spangled with vermilion and emerald green. However glowing his light effects, he kept clear of the sensual frenzy indulged in by the other Fauves; he never yielded to the lure of outright expressionism that tempted them all, but already kept his fervor—as he called it—under steady control. After Matisse's stay at Saint-Tropez in the summer of 1904, with Cross and Signac, Fauvism went through a divisionist phase, surmounted in 1906 under the dominant influence of Gauguin. But with Braque this phase was prolonged (and indeed pointillist beaches often reappeared in his work) until 1907, as is shown by this gem of absolute radiance, the *Little Bay at La Ciotat* (Sidney Janis Gallery, New York), at once crystalline and moiré, dawn-tinted and sunset-colored.

During the summer he was joined by Friesz, who had already worked at La Ciotat in 1905. The two painters turned from the sea to the surrounding hills and modified their approach. In *Landscape at La Ciotat* (Private Collection, France) the horizon has been raised and perspective contracted. The canvas is organized in height, not in depth, in accordance with an upward movement derived from Cézanne, which now became characteristic of Braque's work. Trees, houses and terrain follow each other as a sequence of simplified planes, forming pliable spheres and volutes, yellow, orange and violet edged with red and blue. The necessities of surface patterning are still respected, while the need of organic structure now made itself increasingly felt. Before returning to Paris, Braque, accompanied by Friesz, stopped off at L'Estaque in late September, where his changing approach grew more accentuated. There he began a *View from the Hôtel Mistral* (Mr and Mrs Werner E. Josten Collection, New York), which he finished in Paris. The landscape is disposed between three tall trees, which rise up behind a stone balustrade. A warm tonality continues to prevail, though already there appear the dark greens and browns hitherto taboo. But the role of color now has become constructive rather than decorative. Each form is distinctly bound by thick, unbroken outlines, curving in the case of leafage, elsewhere rectilinear, almost angular. This deliberate concern for geometric construction marks his abandonment of Fauvism and the beginnings of a new orientation. Here too, from a painter trained in the school of Impressionism, we have one of his first works executed from memory, far from the motif; hence its curious tension and the rupture it presages, the transition it marks from the visual attitude to the intellectual, conceptual attitude of Cubism. "My training was naturally all done with a model," declared Braque in a statement of capital importance made to Dora Vallier (*Cahiers d'Art*, October 1954), to which we shall often have occasion to refer. "I learned to paint from life, and when I was finally convinced that I had better get rid of the model, it was by no means easy... But I set to work, and by intuitive stages of growth I managed to detach myself from the model. At times like that one obeys an almost unconscious imperative, there's no telling what will come of it. It's a risky venture."

NUDE, 1907-1908. MADAME MARIE CUTTOLI COLLECTION, PARIS.

THE CUBIST REVOLUTION

So Cubism, now in gestation, though in retrospect remarkable for its regular progression and logical necessity, was originally far less a system than a venture into the unknown. "A methodical venture," Reverdy called it, with Braque in mind, since method was introduced to correct what began as a chance experiment (just as the rule corrects emotion), and since the word "method" must here be taken in its true sense of an orderly course of proceeding, a Cartesian sequence, from *tabula rasa* to the ultimate consequence. Hence the creative force of Cubism and its indelible imprint on our century. In a few inspired years it worked out a new plastic language which overthrew the conventions of several centuries. While Impressionism had revealed a new vision of the world, Cubism founded a new world altogether.

Two decisive revelations were in store for Braque on his return to Paris from the south: Cézanne and Picasso. The achievement of the Aix master was now commanding general attention, especially since his death in October 1906. After paying tribute to him in 1904 and showing his works again in 1905 and 1906, the Salon d'Automne of 1907 organized a large retrospective of Cézanne's paintings and drawings, while a showing of his watercolors was held at the Galerie Bernheim-Jeune. These exhibitions could hardly have been better timed. They created a great stir among the artists of the younger generation, who were ripe for their message. The ascendancy of Cézanne, essentially objective and structural, now supplanted the decorative and sentimental influence of Gauguin. Matisse and Derain had something to do with this change of direction, though it was brought about above all by Braque and Picasso; so that while Cubism marked a break with Fauvism, it also came, at the same time, as a logical sequence in the same chain of events. Two opposing movements they were, but each was bound up with the other and together they contributed to the pulsation of that epoch-making period.

In its two October numbers, moreover, at the very time when the Cézanne retrospective was being held at the Salon d'Automne, the *Mercure de France* published the correspondence between Cézanne and Emile Bernard. One of the last letters (of April 15, 1904), as pithy and mysterious in its phrasing as some fragment from a pre-Socratic philosopher, contains the famous formula which, lifted from its context, was to become an axiom of modern art: "Treat nature in terms of the cylinder, the sphere and the cone." Cézanne was the common source from which many different currents were to flow. Each one of them, tampering with the initial message, only took over and developed parts and particulars of an indissoluble and complex whole. Cézanne would no doubt have had as little sympathy with Cubism as Cubism had with abstract art. It is the fate of genius to set in motion a train of historical events independent of its own aims and achievements. A betrayal as inevitable as it was fruitful, Cubism, by exactly misrepresenting everything he stood for, departed from the outward *aspect* of Cézanne's work the better to penetrate its *essence*, which lies in the autonomy and purity of the picture, in the volumetric tension of the flat surface of the canvas, as solid in its mass as an architectural complex, as alive in all its parts as a living organism. This is why Braque, the closest to him in spirit and his true successor, turned toward Cézanne with so whole-hearted a fervor, taking him not as a model to imitate but as an example to follow.

The second revelation came shortly afterward. Braque was approached by a young dealer, D. H. Kahnweiler, who bought several canvases from him, soon signed a contract for his entire output, and introduced him to Guillaume Apollinaire.

The latter took him to Picasso's studio in the Rue Ravignan, and there he saw *Les Demoiselles d'Avignon*, finished in the spring of that year (1907). Braque was at first bewildered by the boldness and singularity of this vast composition which, in its unbridled expressivity, imperiously combined the seminal influences of Cézanne and above all of Hellenistic painting, Catalan Romanesque frescos, Iberian sculpture and Negro masks. All the affective values of the Blue and Pink Periods were dissolved and converted into plastic energy. The two figures on the right, rough-hewn and streaked with long parallel scorings, suggest space and volume without recourse to either chiaroscuro or perspective, and herald the advent of Cubism, but in a spirit and of a kind not immediately followed up by Picasso. Though doubtful at first, Braque saw the momentous implications of a revolutionary exploit which, at a blow, transcended the naturalistic tradition and displaced the center of gravity from the thing seen to the creative act itself. He then realized, as he later noted in his *Cahier*, that "it is a mistake to imitate what one wants to create," and that the painter's function is not to "reconstitute an anecdote but to constitute a pictorial entity" embodying its own justification.

In December 1907 he began not a composition but a single monumental figure, a standing *Nude* (Mme Cuttoli Collection, Paris), on which he worked throughout the winter. With his palette reduced to blue grays and pinkish browns, with light rendered compact and dense, volumes bound in thick outlines and modeled without chiaroscuro by color hatchings projecting from angular planes, with space foreshortened and dynamized, and anatomical distortions connecting with many different points of view, this, like the *Demoiselles*, was a climacteric painting. Stylistically ambiguous, its contradictions betray an intuitive effort of metamorphosis, a bold experiment doggedly carried out but still beyond his means. A more deliberate work

HOUSES AT L'ESTAQUE, 1908.
HERMANN AND MARGUERITE RUPF FOUNDATION, BERN.

than Picasso's, however, less abrupt in its muffled power, it avoids the overtones of expressionism and primitivism that were then so marked in analogous pictures not only by Picasso, but also by Matisse and Derain. Gauguin had promoted a better understanding, both esthetic and human, of primitive societies in which ethnologists and philosophers were beginning to take an interest. The discovery, from 1905 on, of the arts of Africa and Oceania had the same catalyzing effect—in reverse—on the Fauves and Cubists (and on the German Expressionists) as the discovery of the Far Eastern arts had had on the Impressionists and Symbolists. Those arts were integrated now, as the others had been before, on successive, well differentiated levels. Their influence conspired with that of Cézanne to speed up a transformation already under way, a plastic reconversion based on the primordial efficacy of *structure* and *rhythm*. These two fundamental and constituent notions of Cubism have now become an inherent part of the contemporary consciousness, in the domains of both science and esthetics, and have determined the present-day orientation of anthropology. "Negro masks," acknowledged Braque (who owned several as early as 1908), "opened new horizons to me. They put me in touch with things instinctive, with direct manifestations that ran counter to the false tradition I loathed." Unlike Picasso however, whose temperament was that of a master form-creator, who fell under the spell of Negro art and took over certain of its procedures, Braque's temperament is essentially *painterly*, essentially *lyrical*, and while he absorbed the spiritual content of that art, he owed nothing to it technically. His own revolution proceeded along specifically pictorial lines, in the wake of Cézanne.

In the early summer of 1908 he revisited L'Estaque for the third time. And now, in a style utterly different from that of his previous work there, he painted a series of landscapes of an austere and arresting density. Seen against a pattern of treetrunks, forming pointed arches and sometimes criss-crossing, the compact, strictly geometric masses of doorless, windowless houses rise up tier on tier on the hillsides, like well-trimmed blocks of stone. One is reminded of Cézanne, of the views of Gardanne and the Bibemus quarry, of the Gothic arches of the *Grandes Baigneuses*. Most representative of this new group of works is the famous version of *Houses at L'Estaque* in the Rupf Foundation, Bern; other versions are in the museums of Basel, Copenhagen and New York. Here we have neither linear nor aerial perspective. The horizon rises so high as to blot out the sky whose boundless space would have left a gap in the surface unity. Although the picture keeps closely to the motif—how closely is proved by a photograph of the site, taken by Kahnweiler—sensations are resolutely subordinated to structural requirements, and the painter imposes his own vision on the landscape before him. The result, plainly in contrast with Cézanne, is a dissociation of form and color, which had to be reconquered by successive stages as autonomous picture elements before they could again be unified in accordance with a new rhythm. The initial obsession with volume and absolute structure led to a momentary abandonment of pure color, which would have weakened their intensity.

Rejecting both the impressionist color handling maintained by Cézanne and the artificial, decorative palette of Fauvism, Braque adopted a restrained harmony of cool purplish grays and warm, straw-colored ochres, broken by muted greens; these, at bottom, are the local tones of the stone, soil and trees of Provence. Bright surfaces cutting across dark ones at solid angles of intersection, and each volume thus delimited having its own vanishing point, with no central point of convergence, had the effect of accentuating the stereometric illusion while dispelling the illusion of spatial recession.

STILL LIFE WITH MUSICAL INSTRUMENTS, 1908.
OWNED BY THE ARTIST.

Braque was joined at L'Estaque for part of the summer by
Dufy, while Derain was working near by at Les Martigues.
Derain and Dufy geometrized form, emphasizing the form-
patterns of Cézanne, but without any real innovation of style.
Just as pure tones of flat color do not in themselves amount
to Fauvism if there is no transposition, so nascent Cubism

cannot be equated to geometric structuralization without some metamorphosis of space. The landscapes painted by Picasso late in that same summer in the tiny village of La Rue-des-Bois,

HARBOR IN NORMANDY, 1909.
COLLECTION OF WALTER P. CHRYSLER, JR., NEW YORK.

near Créteil (Oise), point in the same direction, with a certain time-lag, as those painted by Braque at L'Estaque. Picasso's, too, are trees and houses simplified in the extreme, treated in deep greens and browns; but with him the analysis of volume is less thorough and the layout remains static and frontal, with no rupture of perspective. To the influence of Cézanne was now added that of the Douanier Rousseau, whom Picasso and his friends admired with genuine enthusiasm. It was in this very year, 1908, in Picasso's studio in the Bateau-Lavoir, that the famous banquet was held in honor of this unclassifiable master whose earthy naïveté matched the primitive magic of the Negro carvers.

Braque had hitherto exhibited only at the Indépendants, whose doors were open to all. Now he considered his work mature enough to submit to the Salon d'Automne, which had been founded in 1903 in reaction against the promiscuity of the Indépendants, in an effort to marshal the revolutionary forces at work in the ranks of the younger men. It promptly became the rallying point and headquarters of Fauvism. Each elected member of the Salon served in turn on the liberal-minded jury, whose purpose was not so much to eliminate bold and unorthodox efforts as to weed out amateurish and anachronistic work. Each member, moreover, was entitled to "reclaim" an entry rejected by the jury. And though we find the names of Matisse, Rouault and Marquet on the jury of 1908, all six canvases submitted by Braque were rejected; two only were "reclaimed" by Marquet and Guérin. This fact alone eloquently testifies to the heroic isolation in which Cubism took form, and to the radical departure of its innovations. Under these circumstances Braque preferred to withdraw altogether from the Salon d'Automne and accept Kahnweiler's offer of a one-man show in his gallery (27 items, November 9-28, 1908), prefaced by Apollinaire. This show, which in retrospect has become perhaps

LA ROCHE-GUYON, THE CASTLE, 1909.
ROLF DE MARÉ COLLECTION, STOCKHOLM.

the exhibition of the century, attracted little notice at the time; Braque himself kept shyly out of the way, only looking in once shortly before closing day, when there were no more visitors to be seen. One notable critic, however, reviewed the exhibition: Louis Vauxcelles, who three years before had coined the name Fauvism. Now, in the *Gil Blas* of November 14, he used the word "cubes" (suggested no doubt by Matisse) to describe what he saw: "M. Braque is a very bold young man... He despises form and reduces everything, landscapes and figures and houses, to geometric patterns, to cubes." The following spring, referring to two pictures by Braque exhibited at the Salon des Indépendants, Vauxcelles again spoke of "cubic oddities." Before long the terms "cubism" and "cubist" had been coined and become current. They were manifestly applied to Braque in the first instance, and not, as so often supposed, to Picasso, who did not adopt the technique of cubist fragmentation till 1909. By the time Cubism became a fully worked out style, planes had been substituted for volumes and cubes had disappeared. So actually the term is only suitable to the initial phase of the movement (1907-1909), Cézannesque in Braque's work, primitivistic in Picasso's; it aptly serves to emphasize the strongly *tectonic* character of that phase, into which we may certainly read a profound bias toward architecture, whose contemporary revival was directly connected with the rise of Cubism, and possibly also—as suggested by the poet and esthetician Carl Einstein, who published an important study of Braque in 1934—a compensating throw-back to the maternal complex of the house, symbol of refuge and primordial fixation in the midst of the break-down of classical vision.

During the same stay at L'Estaque in 1908 Braque also inaugurated that lifelong series of still lifes, the constant theme of his finest, most characteristic work. With Manet and, above all, with Cézanne, the still life regained its letters of nobility.

It now became the touchstone of Cubism; no theme was better suited to its realist-minded objectivity and its mastery of plastic harmonies. Except for Fernand Léger, who ventured into the mechanical sector, the Cubists made no change in the stock repertory of still life themes. These are always the same familiar objects that go through life with man, answering to his daily needs and essential pleasures: food and drink, the receptacles containing them, tobacco, cards, chessboards, newspapers, books, musical instruments. These last, so often represented in the 17th century—the Golden Age of still life painting—and later by Chardin and Corot, were completely neglected by the Impressionists (except for Degas) and Cézanne. Now they came to hold a privileged place in cubist painting, especially that of Braque, to whom credit must go for reinstating them. Among the still lifes still Cézannesque in structure—pitchers, dishes and bowls of fruit—executed in the latter half of 1908, the *Still Life with Musical Instruments* (owned by the artist) stands out both for the novelty of the theme and its fine mastery of design. Mandolin, clarinet, accordion and score compose a strong and supple harmony of alternately curved and angular masses, answered by the sober color accords of ochres and greens, of cool tones and warm tones. Planes, opened up (the bell of the clarinet), folded back (neck of the mandolin) or raised up (soundbox) to build space and volume with a single movement, ruling out perspective altogether, already show each object far more completely than normal vision does. "Traditional perspective failed to satisfy me. Mechanized as it is, it never puts one in full possession of things." Full possession Braque strove to achieve through a sequence of still lifes whose increasing fragmentation of form led to a temporary neutralization of color.

"What particularly attracted me—and this was the main bearing of Cubism—was the materialization of this new space that I felt to be in the offing. So I began to concentrate on still

GUITAR AND FRUIT DISH, 1909.
HERMANN AND MARGUERITE RUPF FOUNDATION, BERN.

lifes, because in the still life you have a tactile, I might almost say a manual space... This answered to the hankering I have always had to touch things and not merely to see them. It was this space that particularly attracted me, for this was the first concern of Cubism, the investigation of space. Color played only a small part. Light was the only aspect of color that preoccupied us; light and space are two things that bear upon each other and we kept them going together." Braque experimented with them in landscapes, where light varies incessantly and atmospheric space is scarcely reducible to tactile values. He began with some trial landscapes done from memory, the most revelatory of them being the *Harbor in Normandy* (Walter P. Chrysler Jr. Collection, New York), painted in the spring of 1909. Two fishing smacks, with bellying sails, are entering the harbor between two breakwaters, each with a terminal lighthouse. The sky had been eliminated from his L'Estaque landscapes, and trees, houses and terrain echeloned in height, reduced to their primary volumetric forms, with no concern for inner forms. Here sky and sea reappear, but subjected to the same concrete unity of treatment and texture as the other picture elements; and not only is the overall form of each object plainly rendered, but its internal forms are scrupulously detailed, geometrized and patterned in facets. A vivid network of crisscrossing verticals and diagonals thus animates and sustains the composition, distributing light, establishing distances, introducing rhythm into the tangible plenitude of a space which, though not illusionistic, is wonderfully differentiated.

When summer came round again, Braque set out to put his methods to the test. Instead of going south to the Mediterranean, he went down the Seine valley to La Roche-Guyon, near Mantes, where Cézanne had stayed with Renoir in 1885 at the height of his constructive period. The small hill town, crowned with its château, is not without reminiscences of

Gardanne. The houses beneath the castle, its turrets reaching toward the sky, rise in a straggling pyramid through arches of leafage and shrubbery, and this characteristic site inspired Braque to produce a magnificently articulated series of eight landscapes, of a lighter tonality than those of L'Estaque. Suppler volumes, shivered into small fragments in accordance with the system of facets and brought distinctly nearer the spectator, are now traversed by passages, by disrupted outlines, which regularize light by attenuating chiaroscuro effects on the angles of intersection. Late in the summer he moved for a while to Carrières-Saint-Denis with Derain and there painted more landscapes in the same style.

Picasso had been spending his summer holidays in Spain, at Horta de San Juan near Tarragona, and brought back several figure paintings and a series of landscapes, exhibited at Vollard's in November. Converted to Cézannesque methods now, he painted these works in the same spirit, with the same technique, as those of Braque, except that his volumetric crystallization is more pronounced than Braque's, while his palette is reduced to browns and russets, ruling out the atmospheric greens retained by Braque as a means of varying the tones of ochres and grays. Picasso was obsessed by form and its plastic vigor, Braque by space and its pictorial unity. These differences must not blind us to the fact that the two men had been pursuing, independently, parallel lines of research; now they decided to work together, pooling their ideas. Good friends since 1907, they now became inseparable and remained so till the outbreak of war in 1914, setting an example of teamwork probably unparalleled in art history. Cubism passed from its preparatory phase to its high maturity, whose fruitfulness sprang from the conjunction of these two great geniuses, whose opposing gifts contributed to their mutual enrichment. "Braque's temperament was bright, measured, bourgeois; Picasso's dark, extreme, revolutionary.

VIOLIN AND PALETTE,
1909-1910. THE SOLOMON
R. GUGGENHEIM MUSEUM,
NEW YORK.

PIANO AND MANDOLA,
1909-1910. THE SOLOMON
R. GUGGENHEIM MUSEUM,
NEW YORK.

To the spiritual marriage they then contracted," wrote Wilhelm Uhde in 1928, the first man to patronize them both, "one brought a great sensibility, the other a great plastic gift." And alluding recently, not without emotion, to this unique period whose secrets he and Picasso today seem tacitly agreed to share in silence, Braque had only this to say: "We were living in Montmartre, we saw each other every day and talked a lot. Things were said between us in those years that cannot be said again... that no one would understand now... that made us ever so happy. We were like two mountain climbers roped together. We both of us worked very hard... above all we were wholly wrapped up in our work." Picasso's fine portrait of Braque, painted just at this time, in the fall of 1909, testifies to this ardent self-absorption.

At the turn of the century men's relations with the outer world were undergoing a deeper change than at any other time in history, a change amply attested by the parallel metamorphoses of the sciences, of technics, philosophy and all the arts, from architecture to music, from poetry to the cinema. Braque and Picasso were the contemporaries not only of Loos, Joyce and Schönberg, but of Einstein, Bergson and Freud. In all fields of endeavor the real ceased to be a datum and became a process. The fixed and unitary perspective of earlier painting gave place to dynamic articulation, seen from many points of view and rich in unforeseeable combinations. Braque and Picasso sundered the object from its imitative coordinates, and reconstructed it ideally on the two-dimensional surface of the canvas in accordance with the autonomous laws of that surface. They aimed at a total figuration of volume on a plane surface, without illusionism or subterfuge, by means of a system at bottom closer to Egyptian art than to the Renaissance conventions of Alberti. The history of Cubism is the history of the successive solutions they worked out in their efforts to overcome this paradox

GLASS ON A TABLE, 1910.
COLLECTION OF SIR ANTONY AND LADY HORNBY, LONDON.

inherent in painting. The initiative lay now with Braque, more consistent in his approach, now with Picasso, more abrupt in his reactions; but both had to grope for their way, banking on intuition tested by trial and error, not on theories.

PORTRAIT OF A WOMAN, 1910-1911.
COLLECTION OF DR H. CAREY WALKER, NEW YORK.

"Cubism for me, or rather *my* Cubism," Braque confessed, "was a means I worked out for my own use, and its primary purpose was to bring painting within reach of my gifts." After his trips to La Roche-Guyon and Carrières-Saint-Denis, except for occasional views of Montmartre and L'Estaque in 1910 and of Céret in 1911—views of architecture far more than nature—he gave up landscape painting altogether from 1911 to 1928. From Constable to Fauvism by way of Impressionism, landscape, extolled by Ruskin, had been the paramount form of painting in 19th-century Europe. Braque's abandonment of it in favor of figure painting and above all of the still life implied a change of attitude which he justified as follows. "With still life you have a tactile, indeed a manual space, in contradistinction to the visual space of landscape... In tactile space you measure the distance separating you from the object, whereas in visual space you measure the distance separating things from each other. This is what led me, long ago, from landscape to still life." At the time, be it remembered, this notion of an active, tactile space was being investigated by the psychology of perception, and together with the taste for volumetric form, it belonged to the ruling ideas of contemporary esthetics; formulated in 1893 by the German sculptor Hildebrand and brilliantly developed—always in their relation to Renaissance art—by Berenson, these ideas were assimilated by Cubism.

From 1909 on, the breaking up of volume into its component elements by means of faceting was characteristic of what is known as Analytical Cubism. This did not involve the destruction of form, as was generally supposed, but rather a more thorough and complex elaboration of it in terms of the flat surface of the canvas. "When objects shattered into fragments appeared in my painting about 1909, this for me was a way of getting closest to the object, in so far as painting allowed me to do so. Fragmentation helped me to establish space and movement in space, and I couldn't introduce the object till I had created space. At that time I painted a good many musical instruments, first because I was surrounded with them, and secondly because their plasticity and volume fell in with the still life in just the way I wanted... The peculiar thing about a musical instrument, as an object, is that you can bring it to life by touching it." Braque, then, painted not abstractions, but the objects he cared for and lived with, the things that touched him and that he wanted others to see and touch. "A still life ceases to be a still life as soon as it is out of hand's reach."

Foreshadowed in *Guitar and Fruit Dish* (Rupf Foundation, Bern), a perfect synthesis of natural and artificial elements, fragmentation rapidly progressed and gained intensity in the winter of 1909-1910 with *Violin and Palette* and *Piano and Mandola* (both Solomon R. Guggenheim Museum, New York), two admirable pendants, high narrow pictures with a vertical arrangement of multiple facets, each with its own light and its own orientation. Objects spring to life with a single rhythmic impetus, like glittering concretions of space. Curious naturalistic details, like the nail in *trompe-l'œil* from which the palette hangs (and which reappears, this time with no functional justification, in the Basel *Jug and Violin*), or the large candlestick on the piano with its half-consumed candle, emphasize the contrast between the old and the new figuration by putting the reality of the latter to the test. With some small still lifes early in 1910, for example *Glass on a Table* (Hornby Collection, London), presaging the oval form so often to be adopted later, he showed a renewed interest in the structure of the object, but wholly released from classical perspective by *simultaneity* of vision: several aspects of the object are shown at the same time from different angles, without resorting to the use of the mirror which, in the era of nature imitation, from Van Eyck to Manet, was the painter's only way of overcoming the limitations of a single viewpoint.

48

Two misconceptions are still current. In the first place, it was never the aim of Cubism to circle round the object systematically or to define it in terms of descriptive geometry, but rather to evoke its essence and constitutive reality as an indivisible whole. Secondly, time is not meant to be included as a fourth dimension, though it is suggested by this dynamic seizure of tactile space and of the relations linking space to objects.

Braque and Picasso worked apart during the summer of 1910. Braque returned to L'Estaque, while Picasso went down to Cadaquès, in Spain, with Derain. Shattering volumes, Picasso painted austere and grandiose portraits composed of interlocking and *superimposed planes*. Momentarily outdistanced, Braque was soon gaining ground. He in turn tackled the human figure, which he had hitherto neglected—except for a *Woman's Head* (Petit-Palais, Paris) dating from the winter of 1909—but unlike Picasso he never treated it portrait-wise, but only as a pictorial object, undifferentiated from a still life. After two transitional attempts in the summer of 1910, *Woman with a Mandolin* (Chrysler Collection, New York) and *Woman with a Cross* (Bralove Collection, Washington), he made a forward step and entered the so-called hermetic phase of Cubism in the winter of 1910-1911 with the *Portrait of a Woman* (Dr H. Carey Walker Collection, New York). Planes interpenetrate so intricately that there is no distinguishing the discontinuous outlines of the figure from the lines defining the constructive planes. Lighted by projection and not by diffusion, the figure emerges from a schematic network of diagonals and curves. As for color, deliberately suppressed at this stage so as not to "confuse" (as Braque put it) the expression of space, it is reduced to ochres and grays tinged with green and violet.

Braque and Picasso spent the summer of 1911 together at Céret, a charming village in the Roussillon district of the French Pyrenees, which proved to be for Cubism what Collioure,

THE PORTUGUESE, 1911.
KUNSTMUSEUM, BASEL.

MAN WITH A GUITAR, 1911. COLLECTION, THE MUSEUM OF MODERN ART,
NEW YORK. ACQUIRED THROUGH THE LILLIE P. BLISS BEQUEST.

only a few miles away, had been for Fauvism: its privileged place of fulfillment. Stimulated by Picasso, Braque in the course of the year produced four masterly figure paintings: *The Portuguese* (Kunstmuseum, Basel) in the spring, *Man with a Guitar* (Museum of Modern Art, New York) and *Woman Reading* (Raoul La Roche Collection, Paris) in the summer, and *Man with a Violin* (Bührle Collection, Zurich) in the winter. The disintegration of volume had been accomplished. Planes are staggered in the midst of a picture space that has lost its homogeneity and isotropy, where matter has finally ceased to be opaque and is illuminated by transparency and refraction. The harsh rigor of the composition, tightly bound in a pyramidal mesh alternately limpid and mottled, sustains an intense and lofty poetry. Just as the Chardins of the La Caze Collection which entered the Louvre in 1869 had the effect of creating a climate favorable to the still lifes of Cézanne and Manet, so the revelation in Paris in 1909 of Corot's long-neglected figure paintings, with their high proportion of Musicians and Women Reading, no doubt accounts to some extent for Braque's and Picasso's predilection for these themes. Picasso exchanged one of his own portraits in 1910 for a figure painting by Corot, and Braque's veneration for this master is well known; both he and Juan Gris copied some of Corot's figures.

By the end of 1911 Braque had taken to oval and even circular canvases (e.g. *Soda*, Museum of Modern Art, New York), which did away with the empty spaces and dispersal of energy caused by angles, rendering the picture surface more compact and more vibrantly tactile. Rhythmic concentration thus attained its highest intensity. This effervescent phase of his work has no equivalent in that of Picasso. Scenting the danger of obscurantism and abstraction, Braque in the spring of 1912 reverted to serener compositions, better aired, less esoteric. Simplified, outspread planes, lying flush with the

STILL LIFE WITH A BUNCH OF GRAPES, 1912.
D. H. KAHNWEILER COLLECTION, PARIS.

picture surface, rise toward the spectator's eye, while harmoniously articulating space with their differences of value, form, orientation and structure. To this majestic architectonic cadence was added the counterpoint of delicate linear accents in the *Homage to J. S. Bach* (formerly H. P. Roché Collection, Paris), a musical pause in anticipation of the next metamorphosis.

FRUIT DISH AND GLASS, 1912.
PRIVATE COLLECTION, FRANCE.

STILL LIFE WITH PLAYING CARDS, 1913.
MUSÉE D'ART MODERNE, PARIS.

In July 1912 Braque and Picasso again joined forces, this time at Sorgues near Avignon. Their studio, according to Picasso, became a kind of laboratory. They experimented with constructions in metal and paper (none of which survive). After the conquest of space, Cubism's prime achievement— as the conquest of atmosphere was for Impressionism, and the conquest of light for Fauvism—they set out now to reintegrate color, to break out of the impasse of Analytical Cubism. Reactivizing on a creative level the craftsmanship acquired as a house painter, Braque made the decisive innovations by adding allusions to visual reality to the abstract surface of the picture. To him we owe the famous nails in *trompe-l'œil* which appeared in the winter of 1909-1910, then in 1910, and more systematically in the spring of 1911 with *The Portuguese*— inspired by a musician he saw in a bar in Marseilles, the curtain cord on the upper right elliptically evoking the setting—the introduction of numbers and letters of the alphabet, stenciled on the canvas, which contribute their allusive value and, thanks to their broad-based stability unamenable to distortion, serve as reference marks for the plotting out of space. Moved by his deep-seated love of reality, Braque next proceeded to imitate the graining of marble and wood, and to transform the actual physical texture of the picture surface. He mixed sand, sawdust, iron filings and other ingredients with his pigments. The *Still Life with a Bunch of Grapes* (D. H. Kahnweiler Collection, Paris), which also contains letters of the alphabet, was one of the first canvases he painted on a sand ground at Sorgues in the summer of 1912. The quality of the color is directly connected with variations of texture. And though this enrichment of his materials proved to be very fruitful indeed, it was not yet the solution he was aiming at.

"Color came into its own," Braque explained, "with *papiers collés*. This is a fact which critics have never quite grasped.

With these works we succeeded in dissociating color from form, in putting it on a footing independent of form, for that was the crux of the matter. Color acts simultaneously with form, but has nothing to do with form." A few months earlier, by inserting a real object in the painting, a strip of oilcloth simulating the cane bottom of a chair, Picasso had created the first *collage*, a lucky find whose wonderful possibilities did not immediately dawn on him. In September 1912, while Picasso was away on a trip to Paris, Braque, remaining behind at Sorgues, followed up a similar line of research, but with a different end in view, and composed *Fruit Dish and Glass* (Private Collection, France), the first *papier collé,* obtained by the application of three strips of wallpaper imitating the graining of woodwork, each strip linked to the next by a few charcoal strokes. A comparison of this historic prototype with the more elaborate painted version of the spring of 1913, *Still Life with Playing Cards* (Musée d'Art Moderne, Paris), reveals the transition from Analytic to Synthetic Cubism and the all-important mutation brought about by *papiers collés.* Here were elements utterly foreign to "fine painting," whose conventional dignity they undermined by rehabilitating the humblest materials and the spiritual power (not the virtuosity) of the artist; their assimilation called for a whole technical and stylistic reorganization adapted to both their concrete presence and their local color, in short an outright change of method summed up in the significant remark of Juan Gris, the new companion of Braque and Picasso at Céret in the summer of 1913: "Out of a cylinder I make a bottle." Broader, suppler, simplified planes, strictly parallel to the picture surface and uncompromisingly mat, create depth by means of an absolute *frontalization* of space. Form and color detached from volume and light can again coexist within the unitary rhythm of the picture. The break with Renaissance naturalism was made

Bra. 23

ARIA DE BACH, 1913. HENRI LAUGIER COLLECTION, PARIS.

complete by the abandonment of the model and of nature imitation, by the adoption of freely invented plastic "signs," comparable to the metaphors of the poets with whom Braque and his friends were now in close contact (Apollinaire, Max Jacob, Pierre Reverdy). Ceasing to be an aspect of visual reality, an empirical technique, painting became a conceptual esthetic,

THE CLARINET, 1913. PRIVATE COLLECTION, NEW YORK.

an objective and poetic organization of the world, rendering its essence, not its appearance. Nothing better illustrates the splendor and rigor of this new idiom than the *papiers collés* of 1913, so thoroughly stripped of non-essentials, so close in their clean-cut spatial and chromatic relations to some of the latest trends of contemporary painting. *Aria de Bach* (Henri Laugier Collection, Paris) and *The Clarinet* (Private Collection, New York) are two supreme examples, outstanding both for their musical resonance and their full-bodied monumentality. The name of Bach, with its connotation of flawless architecture and pure rhythm, is not invoked in vain.

The technique of *papiers collés* was enriched with a great variety of wallpapers, to which were soon added sheets of music, odd pieces of newspapers and posters, the wrappers from packs of cigarettes and tobacco, matchboxes, labels from bottles, visiting cards, postage stamps, etc., all of which came in for astonishing transfigurations. Picasso in particular took to them with irresistible verve, fancifulness and romantic irony, combining them with drawing and painting. Braque used them more discreetly and literally, combining them only with drawing (pencil, gouache and charcoal) in ways whose plastic rigor by no means ruled out a touch of mystery.

Woman with a Guitar (Musée d'Art Moderne, Paris) of 1913 and its pendant, *Man with a Guitar* (André Lefèvre Collection, Paris) of 1914, are monumental works forming two synthetic interpretations of one of Braque's favorite themes. The first, in gray-green touched up with blacks and browns, and based on the style of his *papiers collés*, still shows traces of Analytical Cubism; the second is fully controlled, form, color and texture enhancing each other. After the rigors of Hermetic Cubism, the same easy freedom imbued all his still lifes, with their relaxed structure and diversified textures, granular, ornamental, often pointillist (*Music*, 1914, Phillips Collection, Washington).

THE MUSICIAN, 1917-1918. KUNSTMUSEUM, BASEL.

Braque got married in 1912 and had hardly settled down at Sorgues with his wife when war broke out in the summer of 1914 and he was called up. Picasso accompanied him to the railway station at Avignon, and there the two friends—whose lines of development were already diverging—parted for good. Braque served with distinction at the front and was twice mentioned in dispatches. Then, in May 1915, he suffered a serious head-wound and had to be trepanned; after several months in hospital, he went back to Sorgues for a long convalescence. In January 1917 his friends threw a banquet to celebrate his recovery and his return to Paris. He took up his brushes again and sought to recapture his old style, aligning himself on Picasso's recent work and above all on that of Juan Gris, for their reciprocal admiration had now brought the two men in close contact. The major work embodying his effort at readaptation, forming a landmark in his career of the same nature and importance as the *Nude* (Madame Cuttoli Collection, Paris) of exactly ten years before, is the large *Musician* (1917-1918, Kunstmuseum, Basel), which represents the fulfillment of Synthetic Cubism and the conclusion of the series, inaugurated in 1910, of figures with musical instruments. Though a trifle stiff, the layout is positively arresting with the broad tracts of flat color, the ornamental background, the solid geometric masonry of the composition, and the masked face of the woman musician emerging from a rich pattern of smooth and dotted planes. His contemporary still lifes, treated in a great variety of formats (rectangular, lozenge-shaped, mandorla-shaped), bring to mind the bas-reliefs of the sculptor Henri Laurens, a friend of Braque and to some extent his disciple. In addition to their exquisite pictorial qualities, they constitute a solid set of *tableaux-objets* (one of the essential aims of Cubism, furthered by *papiers collés*), which can be carried about and will stand up to rough handling.

FRUITION AND VARIATIONS

MATISSE and Picasso, one over-age, the other a Spanish national, were not called up. From Braque, however, the war exacted a heavy ransom. While the essential man remained unchanged, the ordeal through which he passed left its mark on him, deepening his inner life and strengthening the meditative side of his nature. On his sick-bed he wrote his *Pensées et Réflexions sur la Peinture*, published in December 1917 in *Nord-Sud*, a review edited by his friend Reverdy. These ruminations on his art, the key to Braque's esthetic, show him pursuing his constant aim: the identification of appearances and their underlying meaning, of pictorial texture and its poetic value. "The painter thinks in forms and colors; in the object lie his poetics."

By the end of 1918, after feeling his way for several months, Braque had regained full possession of a style which, from now on, developed on its own foundations and reached fruition in many variations. With technical problems solved and a fully constituted syntax, he brought his vision to bear in all its hallucinatory power. The effect of *hallucination*, to which Braque surrendered himself with increasing abandonment—"impregnation, obsession, hallucination," he himself defined the process—was to destroy both the consciousness of the subject and the convention of the object, their false duality, and to restore the world to its shifting interchanges, to the inexhaustible flux of analogies and metamorphoses. The discipline of Synthetic Cubism was reconciled with the spontaneous freshness of objects which seem to close of their own accord with the forms that bring them to life. "My concern," says Braque, "is to put myself in unison with nature rather than to copy her"—or to dominate her, we might add. Gone is the constructive tension of his pre-war work, with its articulated phases. The creative process had become so well attuned to the workings of his

STILL LIFE ON A TABLE, 1918. THE LOUISE AND WALTER
ARENSBERG COLLECTION, PHILADELPHIA MUSEUM OF ART.

STILL LIFE WITH A GUITAR, 1919.
COLLECTION OF MR AND MRS JOSEPH PULITZER, JR., ST. LOUIS.

mind that it was invisible, without either beginning or end, and only his *Carnets de dessins*, begun in 1918 and jealously preserved by the artist, give us some insight into his secrets, into his allusive method of composition.

His new manner emerged in the fall of 1918 with the luxuriant trio of *Still Lifes on a Table*, exhibited in March 1919 at Léonce Rosenberg's gallery, L'Effort Moderne, and now divided between the Philadelphia, Eindhoven and Basel Museums. He had taken up this theme of the *guéridon*, or pedestal table, as early as 1911 (Musée d'Art Moderne, Paris), and Picasso treated it repeatedly from 1919 to 1925. In the coming years, up to 1942, Braque reverted to it in several series of stylistically varied paintings. There even exists a final version (owned by the artist) on which Braque worked intermittently from 1939 to 1952.

His evolution after the First World War no longer followed the methodical progression of the cubist and pre-cubist years. He got into the habit of working on several canvases at the same time, for months and even years, now building them up around a single conception, now branching out into conflicting styles, as the mood took him, sometimes changing pace abruptly, sometimes gradually. So his work no longer evolved through a succession of regular stages, but wound its way along an unforeseeable course like a river in spate, developing in unequal but organically connected cycles which, chronologically, often overlap. His production, moreover, now fell into two distinct categories: small-size canvases easily carried about (chiefly still lifes, a few seascapes after 1928, more recently some landscapes), fine pieces of painting, cabinet pictures in the best tradition of French craftsmanship; and vast, complex ensembles from the brush not only of an unsurpassable executant but of a creator always on the alert for new, unexplored pathways. It is these major sequences, widely scattered and unfamiliar to many, together with several isolated compositions of determinant value, that must be considered before all else if we want to take the measure of Braque's genius and his powers of invention.

An interval of only a few months separates the Philadelphia *Still Life on a Table* from the Basel *Musician*, but what a change! The cubist structures have been softened and humanized, and geometric rigidity smoothed away. Denticular planes and flexuous curves uplift the exuberant mass of objects and tie it in with the participating rhythm of the background elements. The rich pictorial substance unifying form, color and texture attains that plenitude henceforth characteristic of Braque (whose whole future work is herein contained), that singular quality defined as follows by Jean Paulhan: "Fluid (without any need of air), radiant (without any source of light), dramatic (without any pretext)." Picasso set up his colorful *Guéridons* in front of a window open on the sky of Dinard or Saint-Raphaël. Braque, as much at home in a rigidly confined space as Chardin, opened no windows in his painting before 1938 (Juan Gris had already done so by 1915, Picasso by 1919); he opened no windows, that is, until he had progressively, tactilely conquered the corresponding space of the room. Issuing from the movement of tones alternately warm and cool, bright and dark, light is not so much an external illumination as a muted phosphorescence emanating from objects and bound up with the quality and materiality of color. And color, deliberately attenuated in a confined, almost nocturnal space, gains in indefinite depth what it loses in brilliance: "Blacks and browns, all those tones that enter into the luxuriant fur of wild beasts, glow in the darkness like the lamps of a sanctuary" (Jean Grenier).

Along with the *Guéridon* paintings came a rich flowering of still lifes. The vertical layout of the former was swung over and the same objects were displayed horizontally on a table, in a rectangular, much elongated picture format peculiar to Braque, which he used to fine effect. With consummate craftsmanship, he alternated thick and thin coats of paint, mat and lustrous passages, smooth and granular surfaces, incorporated sand and even plaster in his pigments, and deftly worked in letters of the alphabet. After establishing the form-color-texture relationship and liberating the sinuosities of line, he reverted to arrangements of flat surfaces, "in order to gauge the amplitude of color, as Braque himself put it."

The remarkable *Still Life with a Guitar* (1919, Pulitzer Collection, St. Louis) is painted on the black ground he used so often from 1918 to 1926, which accentuates spatial depth and the resonance of colors set off by warm sustaining passages of white. The stylized bunch of grapes, a familiar presence since the days of Cubism, often accompanies musical instruments, and there may well be a hidden meaning behind the frequency with which

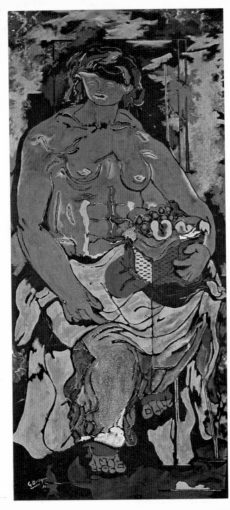

NUDE WOMAN WITH BASKET OF FRUIT (CANEPHORUS), 1926.
NATIONAL GALLERY OF ART, WASHINGTON, D.C. (CHESTER DALE COLLECTION)

THE MANTELPIECE, 1925.
COLLECTION OF MR AND MRS SAMUEL A. MARX, CHICAGO.

GUITAR AND FRUIT, 1927.
COLLECTION OF MR AND MRS M. LINCOLN SCHUSTER, NEW YORK.

they go together. "In the guitar," Juan Gris used to say, "Braque found his new Madonna." And grapes, Hegel tells us, in addition to the sensual purity of their form, are the nearest equivalent of the ideal color of the feminine complexion. By virtue of its composition and execution, Braque's painting is essentially musical; its affinities in fact, as has often been pointed out, lie more particularly with chamber music. If his cubist pictures, thanks to the compelling rigor of the theme, may be likened to a fugue, the works painted after 1918, with their looser articulation and vast horizontal or vertical surfaces punctuated with recalls and caesuras, are more like sonatas. Bach was followed by Mozart, and indeed the very word "sonata" figures on one of these still lifes of the 1920s (Petit-Palais, Paris), so rich in musical inscriptions of both an allusive and a constructive value.

In 1922 Braque was forty. The Salon d'Automne devoted a special room to his work in recognition of his achievements. He embarked on the double series of *Canephori* (Basket Bearers) and *Mantelpieces*, pursuing them simultaneously till 1927. These are complementary expressions of the same monumental classicism, for the high cheeks of the fireplace supporting the crowded mantelshelf are no less majestic than the human figure treated as a caryatid. "No one is less concerned than he is with psychology, and I fancy a stone moves him as much as a face does." This often-quoted comment of Apollinaire, originally applied to the early work, was truer than ever of the pictures painted in the twenties, for it points up the fact that by now Braque had overcome anthropomorphism, that for him humanity had resolved itself into universality. Soberly draped nudes, sturdy column-figures crowned with capitals, these stately offering bearers or canephori magnify womankind and all life, and evoke the ancient goddesses of fecundity. Full-bodied forms and swelling curves are suggested by bright or dark color patches against the brownish red of the flesh tints, and by a curious kind of blue-print drawing invented by Braque. The figures are presented either standing, with a basket of fruit on their shoulder, as in the fine initial pair of 1922 (Musée d'Art Moderne, Paris); or seated, sometimes half-length, with the basket resting against their hip; or reclining, without the basket, like bathers. Among many variants of unequal value, some less firmly designed than

THE ROUND TABLE, 1929. PHILLIPS COLLECTION, WASHINGTON, D.C.

STILL LIFE: LE JOUR, 1929. NATIONAL GALLERY OF ART,
WASHINGTON, D.C. (CHESTER DALE COLLECTION).

others, though all are imbued with a decorative stateliness, the
finest is the Canephorus *(Nude Woman with Basket of Fruit)*
of 1926 in the Chester Dale Collection, Washington, outstanding
for its power and robust vigor—a statue of the Grand Siècle for
the gardens of Versailles, seen here against the marble ground
employed in the *Mantelpieces.*

HERAKLES, 1931. INCISED PLASTER. AIMÉ MAEGHT COLLECTION, PARIS.

The four major versions of the *Mantelpieces* date from 1922 (Weil Collection, St. Louis), 1923 (Kunsthaus, Zurich), 1925 (Marx Collection, Chicago) and 1927 (Norton Gallery, West Palm Beach, Fla.). They continue the vertical format of the *Guéridons*, with a different architectonic support and with a texture of imitation marble instead of imitation wood graining. The composition is organized in two zones: in the upper half of the canvas (to which the eye is drawn at once, as so often in Braque's pictures since the L'Estaque landscapes) is a colorful profusion of objects and undulating forms built up in staggered planes on the cubist principle; in the lower half is the great rectangular empty space of the fireplace, more naturalistically rendered. This bold conjunction of two systems of representation, magisterially interconnected, permits of the complete expression of a continuous picture space, now empty, now full, a space both visual (distance from one object to another suggested by drawing them apart) and tactile (distance from objects to the spectator suggested by drawing them together). Take the version in the Marx Collection, Chicago (sometimes dated to 1922), perhaps the most harmonious of this amazing group of pictures. Against the wallpapers of the background fixing the limit of the canvas, the cubist still life, as the central point of attraction, is laid out on three successive planes: score and fruit dish with pears; bottle; fruit dish with grapes and guitar. The high, plunging line of sight and the weight of the objects distend the mantelshelf, whose volutes are both the support and the rhythmic extension of the still life. The slant of the mantelpiece, together with the sharp recess of the white fireplace and the black register, emphasizes the suggestion of space and brings objects forward, "within hand's reach." The *Marble Table* (1925, Musée d'Art Moderne, Paris) is a fascinating variant of the *Mantelpieces*, with tactile space predominating. Fruit and objects (the cithara of antiquity has replaced the guitar) glow like idols on a marble slab with veinings reminiscent of the skies of Toledo as we see them in El Greco. The black and white tablecloth slipping over the dark green panel laid slantwise across the table awakens strangely deep-toned harmonies, and even more so than in the *Mantelpieces* we sense an uneasy equipoise, about to give way, as in the 17th-century Dutch still life which Claudel aptly described as "an arrangement in process of disintegrating, something a prey to duration."

With the *Canephori* and the *Mantelpieces*, and the admirable still lifes that go with them, all the senses are roused to full enjoyment of luscious fruit and full-blown flowers, disregarded by Cubism but now given their due; of *Anemones* above all (1925), variations of color on the same broad and flexible form; of earthenware and stoneware vessels; of the ever-recurring musical instruments. With all these themes Braque's aim was to bend texture to his will with a velvet touch, "to see how far one could go in the alliance of volume and color." This period of reconciliation between elements that the technique of *papiers collés* had once served to dissociate or reduce was not to last long, for each phase of a living evolution leads to its own destruction, i.e. to renewal. But this period corresponds to Braque's high maturity and gave birth to several masterpieces which have nothing in common with the contemporary achievements of Picasso (Juan-les-Pins series of 1924-1925) and take their place in the characteristically French lineage of Chardin, Courbet and Cézanne.

The transition took place in 1927 with some still lifes of an austere and vigorous splendor, tempered by the insertion of a decorative branch of leafage. The most famous of these is the *Black Rose* (Tremaine Collection, Meriden, Conn.), which figured in the great Still Life Exhibition at the Orangerie, Paris, in 1952; the most curious and the most soundly designed is *Guitar and Fruit* (Schuster Collection, New York), which we reproduce.

Here we see, first, the intense radiation of black used as a total color and a spiritual force; secondly, the generalization of a technique which Cubism had initiated and which Braque had practised since the war: the vertical division of objects and of the main picture elements into two halves, one dark, one light, This was a further application of the principle of simultaneity, a means of suggesting volume by flat colors without either shading or chiaroscuro. If in the natural world "to render light... presupposes a half-share of bleak shadow" (Valéry), in the pictorial world of Braque the zone of shadow is no less vivid than the zone of light; here, with their forthright contour lines, both have the same positive value, stand out as dense and fluid color patches, fit together like earthenware tiles, and bring to mind "the firm freshness of Late Empire mosaics in which shadows appear to be welded to the bodies that project them" (Charles Sterling).

Bringing with them a succession of important changes, the years 1928-1932 mark a period of intensive experiment in both themes and techniques, the results of which could be seen at the large exhibition held at Basel in the spring of 1933. With the series of *Guéridons* he began in 1928, many of them (e.g. Museum of Modern Art, New York) even taller and narrower pictures than those of 1918-1919, and with the corresponding still lifes, Braque abandoned the thick impasto, the sonorous black grounds and the inflected brushwork he had hitherto cultivated. Instead, on a granular ground of gesso mixed with sand, rich in tactile qualities, he spread a coat of paint as thin and mat as that of a fresco. After the grave harmonies of deep-toned grays, greens and browns of the past decade, there came now a limpid, lightened, evenly distributed scale of bright blues, greens and yellows, of ochres and tan, quickened by sharp contrasts (no longer soft and velvety) of smooth blacks and whites. Instead of clashing with a restricted neutral ground,

BROWN STILL LIFE, 1932. OWNED BY THE ARTIST.

objects expand within a larger compass, within an actual room where light circulates freely (and thin strips of unpainted canvas also allow color to breathe freely), and where the wall surfaces recede and take definite shape. As before, the picture is built up solely around an arrangement of flat, unmodeled surfaces, but a sense of volume and space is conveyed by the distribution of curved and rectilinear masses, by the realistic rendering of wall ornaments and the legs of tables, and above all by the systematic vertical bisection, amplifying the angular fold of the scores over the whole canvas. *The Round Table* (1929, Phillips Collection, Washington) is no doubt the most powerful and best orchestrated of these new *Guéridons*. The sweep of the eye takes in and appreciates the surface expanse recently conquered by the painter, as it glances up first at the roughly sketched ceiling, then lingers over the circular rhythm of the still life straight in

STILL LIFE, 1934. EMANUEL HOFFMANN FOUNDATION, KUNSTMUSEUM, BASEL.

front of it, and finally drops down to the floor whose geometric pattern offsets the splendid curve of the round table. In the related still lifes of the same period, rectangular in shape but magnified by the impetus of powerful verticals, like the one in the Sacher Collection, Basel, or *Le Jour* in the Chester Dale Collection, Washington, which number among the finest of the century, in no way inferior to the most brilliant of Matisse and Picasso—in these still lifes the background ornamentation extends to the entire wall surface, including both wainscoting and wallpaper. This proliferation of ornamental motifs was to increase as time went on; their purpose, as Braque himself pointed out, was again to sever form from color and to open up new possibilities of line.

In 1925 Braque moved into the handsome, well-lit Paris house built for him near the Parc Montsouris by the architect Auguste Perret. After 1926 he ceased to spend his holidays at Sorgues and soon gave up the Midi altogether. In 1929 he went back to Normandy and in 1931 bought a country house, in the style of the region, at Varengeville near Dieppe. There he painted some small seascapes which, if not of major importance in his output, have nevertheless an undeniable charm and, behind their decorative transpositions, give a wonderfully accurate rendering of the Channel coast, with its softly molded cliffs edging out between a lowering sky and dark seas, with boats stranded on the pebbly beach—moments of relaxation between more ambitious and complex works.

He also reverted to the human figure, with a series of *Heads*, some divided into two distinct halves (1929) on the principle of his still lifes, some with two juxtaposed profiles (1929-1930). Then, surely acting on Picasso's example as given in his convulsive Dinard beach scenes of 1928, he produced two series of *Bathers* subjected to strange and provocative distortions. The first (1930), with tiny heads and bodies triangulated by a kind of cubist segmentation, are lying on the sand. The second, wavy masses and enveloping curves expressing the erotic essence of femininity, are grouped two by two, one reclining, one standing. For all the ingenuity that went into them, these complex and outlandish exercises (perhaps the only ones with a trace of Expressionism) are not always entirely successful and Braque himself recently saw fit to destroy some of them and recast several others. But the researches they imply were not carried out in vain. The ambiguous, curvilinear forms of these *Bathers* sometimes recur long afterwards in the wavering contours of the *Cliffs* (1938, Block Collection, Chicago). They recur too, up to 1934, in the familiar objects of a group of simplified still lifes in which fine white outlines are delicately incised in a thin coat of paint reduced to tonalities of brown, green, black and Indian red; the finest are those in the Penrose Collection at Chiddingly (1931), in the artist's own collection (1932) and in the Emanuel Hoffmann Foundation, Basel (1934). These studies of rhythms and curves, moreover, directly paved the way for the linear neo-classic style which he made into the accomplished vehicle of his decorative work. By no means a virtuoso, he constantly needs to feel the resistance and, conversely, the solicitation of his materials. The art form—an invention of his own—that best crystallized his graphic work at this period was incised plaster, with sharply cut white lines running like hieroglyphics over the coat of black paint covering the plaster. This technique was derived from the glyptic art of the 18th century and above all from ancient models that Braque wholeheartedly admired: the designs on Greek seals and vases and Etruscan bronze mirrors. His inspiration was drawn from mythological sources rediscovered by instinct and particularly suited to this technique. Christian Zervos, as an enthusiastic admirer of both modern art and the ancient arts of the Mediterranean, has attempted several times to show what binds Braque so closely to archaic

THE YELLOW TABLECLOTH, 1935.
COLLECTION OF MR AND MRS SAMUEL A. MARX, CHICAGO.

Greece and what separates him from it just as radically. His first incised plasters, four large panels representing ancient heroes and goddesses like *Herakles* and *Io* (now in the Maeght Collection, Paris; smaller variants, of 1932, in the Sacher Collection, Basel), were conceived in 1931-1932 as decorations for an apartment in Paris. They coincided with the execution of the etchings illustrating Hesiod's *Theogony* and initiated a series of decorative works, as numerous as they are technically varied, ranging from engraving to sculpture, to which he is still adding today.

From 1933 to 1938 Braque's evolution was marked by a sequence of decorative still lifes based on a lavish horizontal layout rather than on a firm vertical structure. He kept to the same objects, guitar, fruit dish, score, glass and bottle, arranged

THE PURPLE TABLECLOTH, 1936.
COLLECTION OF MRS ALBERT D. LASKER, NEW YORK.

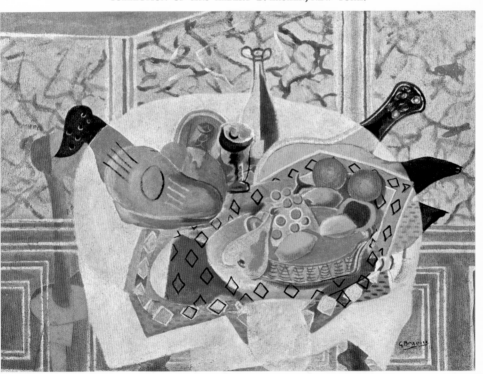

STILL LIFE WITH A MANDOLIN, 1938.
COLLECTION OF MR AND MRS LEIGH B. BLOCK, CHICAGO.

on the cloth of round or rectangular tables but swept up now
in an unforeseen flux of metamorphoses and located in an
increasingly ornamental spatial setting. *The Pink Tablecloth* (1933,
Chrysler Collection, New York) is built up around a central
ellipse and interlocking curves which govern the background
and bulge out to form a vigorous, sensuous, fully tactile space.

The surface texture of oil paints mixed with sand has become thick and heavy, and sonorous carmines, violets and yellows accompany the dominant pink patterned with sinuous blacks. *The Yellow Tablecloth* (1935, Marx Collection, Chicago), which won the Carnegie Prize at Pittsburgh in 1937, is conversely a tissue of aerial paleness and subtle diagonals defining a clear visual space. From a low angle of vision the spectator's eye swings rapidly upward through the empty space, taking in the table with its divergent edges, and comes to rest on the molding of the ceiling where the elongated spiral of the guitar finally vanishes. The miracle is that so translucid a work should be so mysteriously baffling. The panels of the wainscoting are delicately decorated, but the wall above, treated in airy violet grays, is quite plain. In *The Purple Tablecloth* (1936, Lasker Collection, New York) all the walls are papered or wainscoted. The objects projecting beyond the table are darker in color, thus setting off the circular movement of the tablecloth and the beautifully rounded shape of the still life against the slanting wall panels of the room.

Braque's keenly imaginative decorative sense reached its height in 1938 with the *Still Life with a Mandolin* (Block Collection, Chicago), so skillfully controlled in its magnificence and complexity. Except for the mandolin itself, thus made to stand out as a pure ornament, flexible as a swan, nothing escapes the decorative contamination which weaves an unbroken web of arabesques and flourishes, entwining and deforming objects. "Echo answers to echo," as Braque puts it, "everything reverberates," by associations, contrasts and metaphors. Space, whose apparently arbitrary rhythmic saturation is justified by necessities other than merely decorative, is thus in a state of ceaseless movement and fusion—what Braque calls the "picture climate." "A certain temperature must be reached, high enough to make things malleable." They then tend to lose their identity and to enter the infinitely variable cycle of correspondences that now increasingly came to govern Braque's painting (and thought). Compositional homogeneity is ensured by a freedom of handling that espouses the modulations of texture, and by the all-pervading mildness of a color scheme relieved, nevertheless, by sharp accents of red and black.

CLIFFS, 1938. COLLECTION OF MR AND MRS LEIGH B. BLOCK, CHICAGO.

In order to humanize and control this decorative exuberance, Braque executed from 1936 to 1939 (and occasionally up to 1944) a series of figure compositions, or more exactly interiors, in which the human figure appears as an important element (vertical and mobile)—but by no means all-important—of spatial organization. These works come under the heading of genre painting as regards their subject matter, but the spirit imbuing them is not that of genre painting, for anecdote is entirely absent and the human figure depersonalized. The notion of portraiture is utterly foreign to Braque's art, not only because (as he himself explains it) his temperament is not masterful enough, but also because he thinks and works in terms of universality, not of individuality. There is nothing here of the emotional tension or sensual delight that characterize analogous themes in the hands of Matisse and Picasso. Figures, mainly female, appear singly or in pairs in the guise of musicians or painters, thus embodying Braque's two muses, whose powers merge in his inspiration. Like the objects in his still lifes, they are usually divided vertically into two halves, one in shadow, one in light. Is there, as some seem to think, a hidden meaning behind this division? To begin with, this was doubtless no more than a technical device taken over from Cubism, a means of suggesting volume and movement in the flat silhouettes of these figures, by evoking several aspects of them simultaneously. Underlying this phenomenon, nevertheless, is the principle of a fundamental ambiguity: that of body and soul, of man in search of his double and, in the dramatic versions of the war years, of the specter of death embracing life. Outstanding among the pictures with a single figure are several interpretations of the *Woman Painting* (1936, Cummings Collection, Chicago; 1937, Marx Collection, Chicago, and Delubac Collection, Paris) and the *Woman with a Mandolin* (1937, Museum of Modern Art, New York). A dark silhouette with phosphorescent fringes incised with white lines, as in the

WOMAN WITH A MANDOLIN, 1937. COLLECTION, THE MUSEUM
OF MODERN ART, NEW YORK. MRS SIMON GUGGENHEIM FUND.

engraved plasters, the woman with a mandolin is seen in profile against the picture plane, while the ornamental planes of the background recede behind her. The suffocating atmosphere of the surrounding space is full of lights and sounds. The score on the pedestal balancing the woman's elongated torso and suggesting spatial recession, together with the still life on the upper left among the wallpapers, forming a painting within the painting—

THE PAINTER AND HIS MODEL, 1939.
COLLECTION OF WALTER P. CHRYSLER, JR., NEW YORK.

THE STUDIO, 1939. PRIVATE COLLECTION, NEW YORK.

these are touches of an incomparable pictorial quality. If the
Woman with a Mandolin brings to mind Corot, the *Duet* (1937,
Musée d'Art Moderne, Paris), typical of Braque's two-figure
compositions, is as luminous and flawlessly designed as an
interior by Vermeer, an effect obtained however not by
crystallization but by emanation.

Two major works painted in 1939, both representing his studio, one with, the other without figures, brilliantly summed up all the experiments carried out since Cubism and at the same time foreshadowed the developments to come. In *The Painter and his Model* (Chrysler Collection, New York) the two figures are built up obliquely in space on either side of the easel, after the manner of the musician and the singer on either side of the piano in the *Duet* of 1937. Sitting in a chair, holding his palette, the painter looms up as a dark profile sharpened by his cigarette and pointed beard. The nude model is seen in three-quarter view, her face shown partly in one color frontally, partly in another color in profile, while the curves of her body are drawn in bright strokes after the manner of the *Canephori*. The lyre-shaped easel with its imitation wood graining holds a small many-colored canvas on which the model is outlined in white. The wall decoration, enhanced by a mirror, forms a vast pentagon with composite ornaments in violently contrasted lighting. In *The Studio* (Private Collection, New York) the figures have been eliminated as, in the last resort, needless and even obtrusive; the spatial rhythm which is Braque's essential concern thus becomes all the more pure and intense. In addition to the luminous rectangle of the window (which introduces, however, no atmospheric diffusion), the principal innovations are the abandonment of a central point of attraction (which had still governed even the recent interiors with two figures) and the harmonious distribution of objects in height and breadth. The composition, with its rich variety of textures, is a tissue of narrow vertical planes broken by diagonals, like those formed by the brushes. The leaves in the vase on the upper left merge into the wall decoration. The star-shaped form on the right, standing out against the easel, is the first intimation of the bird that was to appear ten years later in the great symphonic interiors, of which this canvas is a brilliant anticipation.

PATIENCE, 1942. COLLECTION OF MR AND MRS SAM JAFFE, BEVERLY HILLS, CALIFORNIA.

SPIRITUALITY OF MATTER
AND THE POETICS OF SPACE

B RAQUE was at Varengeville, near Dieppe, in May 1940 when the Germans invaded France. He took refuge for the next few months in the Limousin, then in the Pyrenees; but feeling uprooted and homeless so far from his studio he returned to Paris in the fall and remained there throughout the occupation. The pressure of events checked his momentum for a while and deflected his painting into more direct and expressive channels. Biding his time Braque fell back on his unfailing grasp of sound craftsmanship and communed with the objects around him. Wartime restrictions and confinement to his own home heightened his sense of the humble domestic reality that his painting had always reflected. Like his friend the poet Francis Ponge in those same years, he freely surrendered to the "predestination of things," and feeling himself but a thing among things he listened hard to their whispering voices and divined their secret tenor and common truth.

His decorative vein was not exhausted, and several broadly handled still lifes, built up around a banjo instead of the usual guitar or mandolin, make a rich display of volutes against a patterned background (Madame Frigerio Collection, Paris, and Pulitzer Collection, St. Louis). But the significant works of the years 1939-1941 (and even beyond, up to 1944) feature not so much musical instruments and decorative objects as the strictly rationed necessities of life, a glass of wine, a loaf of bread, a piece of cheese, seen in the light of hard times in all their Biblical dignity, lying there in the frugal company of two or three pieces of fruit, a knife, a pitcher, a soup tureen. Thrift had followed abundance; freed from the intricate toils of ornament, these common domestic objects regained their full weight, their substance and autonomy, presented a little to one side, lighted up and modeled in curving planes against a background wall whose geometric bands give rhythm to the horizontal elongation of the canvas. Sober, varied shades of brown and yellow, gray and black, infuse the granular fibres of the surface texture. The best of these still lifes, so moving in their accuracy and simplicity, were exhibited at the 1943 Salon d'Automne and reproduced in the first edition (1945) of Jean Paulhan's book *Braque le patron*, which he aptly concludes as follows: "I should be at a loss to say whether Braque is the most inventive or most versatile artist of our time. But if the great painter is the one who gives the keenest, most nutritive idea of painting, then for me there is no hesitating: Braque is the master."

In 1942, a singularly fruitful year, Braque recovered the fullness and variety of his inspiration. "I am," he says, "very sensitive to the surrounding atmosphere," and if his allusions to wartime conditions were always indirect, an unconcealed anxiety weighed on his painting now, in sharp contrast with its pre-war serenity. Instead of pleasant, comfortable interiors, he portrayed the utilitarian parts of the house and their scanty furnishings, the unheated bedroom, the bathroom with its bare shelves, the kitchen with its meager supplies and poor array of utensils, and the windows opening now and then on oppressive skies only make the atmosphere bleaker and more austere.

But he did not confine himself to one vein, and in the spirit of his pre-war work he executed three new *Guéridons*, one red and square in format (Private Collection, u.s.a.), another blue, green and black in front of a window (Private Collection, Milan), the last pink with violet overtones (Blondin Collection, Paris). But their ostensibly joyful note is a little forced or muffled. More in keeping with his real feelings, while following the vertical style of the *Guéridons*, are several austere interiors in cold, funereal colors, showing modest deal tables with objects of everyday use: *The Washstand* (two versions, one owned by the artist), seen against a threatening sky, with its reversed perspective powerfully drawing the spectator into the picture; and better yet, *The Kitchen Table* (two versions: Jean Paulhan Collection, Paris, and Gustav Zumsteg Collection, Zurich), which attains to the sublime in its stark fervor, almost like a Jansenistic Chardin. Still other outstanding canvases date from this productive year: a *Woman in Half-length* with ambivalent profiles, one dark, one light, against a marine background, the mysterious conclusion magnified to cosmic dimensions of the 1929-1930 series; *Patience* (Jaffe Collection, Beverly Hills), dramatically harking back to the figure compositions of 1936-1939; and the great *Interior with Palette* (Private Collection, U.S.A.), which forms the connecting link between the original *Studio* of 1939 and the *Studio* sequence of 1949-1956.

A woman playing a game of patience sits uneasily in a closely confined room, amid an inextricable maze of lines and colors, before an opaque window; a tall haggard figure, torn between anguish and hope, with a front view of her face in light and the profile in sinister darkness, her skeletal hand hovers fitfully over the cards on the narrow, coffin-shaped table. *Interior with Palette*, one of his finest works, proposes a tremulous harmony of gray-greens and pinkish grays against a black ground scored with white. The straight-backed chair, painted bright green, offsets the curves of palette and plant; one of the legs merges with the legs of the two-tone table, while a slight shadow detaches the back of the chair from the wall. The transparent forms visible in the foreground, shaped like the horns of a lyre, correspond to the extremities of the easel: through them the painter's eye (and our own) seems to gaze in all directions and explore the endless circuit of this spatial symphony. Some small still lifes of an elongated format complete the cycle: a series of *Teapots* with assorted objects (a version with apples belongs to Picasso)

Bra. 44

THE KITCHEN TABLE, 1942-1943. GUSTAV ZUMSTEG COLLECTION, ZURICH.

and of *Fish*, among them the famous *Black Fish* (Musée d'Art Moderne, Paris), Braque's most popular canvas, its forms and colors reduced to an absolute simplicity, like nothing in the world around us certainly, but more real in a sense because they are archetypes of art and nature, bearing the sovereign mark of their creator.

In 1943 Braque kneaded his still lifes in a thick impasto, with richer, mellower colors, orange-yellows and blue-greens. Objects are seen in close-up within a foreshortened picture space, against dense, vermiculated backgrounds *(The Green Rug*, Musée d'Art Moderne, Paris). This thickly clotted texture reoccurs in a series of *Vanitas* pictures, inaugurated in 1938 in another style. This theme was taken up for plastic and tactile, not for religious reasons; or if the latter seem to be present, it is an unsought-for effect produced by the quality of the execution. Roughly and ruggedly molded, the death's head, crucifix and pitcher substituted here for the rosary (Private Collection, U.S.A.) seem almost like reliefs.

Braque, as a matter of fact, was now experimenting with sculpture. Since Daumier's time, and today above all, many painters have made a point of trying their hand at sculpture. With Matisse (up to 1933) and, even more continuously and boldly, with Picasso, painting and sculpture went hand in hand on the same creative level. Braque, feeling the sculptor's art essentially incompatible with his gifts as a "pure painter," long resisted the temptation. In 1912, when Cubism reached a turning point, he made some paper reliefs (no longer in existence) which were not without influence on the "constructions" of his friend Henri Laurens. A painter—as Laurens has said, with Braque in mind—takes up sculpture out of curiosity to see what really goes on behind his picture. Except for a circular vase (1940), to which he added a curious animal's head, and his earliest surviving plaster statuette, a *Standing Nude* of 1920 which

INTERIOR WITH PALETTE, 1942. PRIVATE COLLECTION, U.S.A.

reduces the curves of the female form to a strictly geometric
structure of lozenges, Braque has not ventured into the field
of sculpture in the round and modeling. Keeping always to
the echeloned planes of Cubism, nearly all his attempts at
sculpture had so far consisted of "profiles" (this was in fact
the title he uses for several of them) in very slight relief.
As for the plaster slabs incised on a black ground, which
he inaugurated in 1931 and has since followed up with others

in relief, sometimes polychromed, these (along with the *papiers collés*) are his most original invention, but they come under the heading of glyptics rather than statuary.

It was during the summer of 1939, on the beach at Varengeville, that Braque first really tackled the problems of sculpture.

THE SALON, 1944. MUSÉE D'ART MODERNE, PARIS.

He carved the soft chalk of the Channel cliffs, assembled stones and bones picked up in the course of his rambles along the beach, and in his Paris studio, which he had fitted up accordingly, he produced a series of statues for casting. He carried on during the war and the occupation, when colors were hard to obtain, not only as a diversion from painting but also out of his love for concrete materials and his need to feel under his grasp the tactile plenitude of objects—a need, an obsession, underlying all his work. His sculptures keep to several main themes to which he returns again and again: the *Horse's Head* (1943), the series of Ponies represented entire or reduced to the head alone, Fish, Birds, human profiles, the Plow, the Vase, Plants (i.e. the kingdoms of nature), symbols of the elements, objects of daily use and implements, simple figures taking the measure of space, setting the rhythm of works and days, imposing a familiar theogony. Decorative sculpture in the best sense of the term, medium-sized and archaic in inspiration (sometimes combining reminiscences of Greek and Chinese art), these works, like everything Braque does, are also spiritual emblems charged with a radiant poetry. The same is true of the color lithographs produced in large numbers since the war, often on parallel themes; without really renewing the technique of engraving, like some of Picasso's recent attempts, the distinction of their style and the savor of a texture as full-bodied as oil paints make them admirable *objets d'art*, among the most accomplished of our time.

In September 1944, just after the liberation of Paris, Braque went back to Varengeville for the first time since the fateful summer of 1940. *The Salon* (Musée d'Art Moderne, Paris) celebrated the return of peace and normal conditions of life. This is the first painting to render a full and natural expression of the space contained within the four walls of a room, open nevertheless on the outside world, with the tender gray-blue sky of the Ile-de-France visible through the half-open window, while the milk-white streak of the other half suffices to differentiate the inner space and the outside light in the simplest, most effective way. With its rectangular frame and the curves of the balcony, this window is the backbone of the composition. The small lozenge-shaped table with its checkered, pearl-gray top valiantly balances the large black table with its sparse, lovingly handled still life. How exquisite are the blue notes of the flowers against the grave, unruffled harmony of the black, white-edged table-top, of the all-pervasive grays, of a brown whose supreme distinction belongs to Braque alone—the brown of walnuts, Havanas, khaki, chestnuts, tobacco, cream, chocolate, and how much else besides! A humanized space breathes here nobly, calmly, with none of the tension implied by the vivid presence of figures in the analogous interiors of Matisse, which this one brings to mind.

Also in 1944 Braque initiated the series of *Billiard Tables*, interrupted by illness, in which the articulation of space, while equally convincing, is markedly bolder. The first version (Musée d'Art Moderne, Paris), with its majestic and inevitable geometry, is unquestionably one of the pinnacles of French art. Against the vast bare rectangle of the broken wall, from which it is separated by the greatly broadened belly of a crystal vase with a cluster of tall leaves, the tilted rectangle of the billiard table in turn is bent, along the same vertical angle as the wall (as hitherto in the *Guéridons*), and made to swing out toward the spectator. The cue lying athwart the table exactly measures the distance between the plane of vision, indicated by the outlined lyre-shaped tips of the easel (which we noted in the *Interior with Palette* of 1942), and the latticed window in the background. Two of the severest of colors, green and brown, clash contrapuntally, heightened by the poetic blue of the sky seen through the window and the bright red of the billiard balls.

In 1945 Braque executed another version, the *Small Billiard Table* (Roland, Browse and Delbanco Collection, London), and two figures of bewildering complexity: *Woman with a Book* (Soulas Collection, Paris) and *Woman at her Toilette* (Private Collection, New York). Then an operation followed by a long convalescence interrupted his work for several months. Taking up his brushes again, he reverted to a series of flower pictures begun in 1942, and more particularly to a series of *Sunflowers* in unctuous yellows begun in 1944, of which the major version (owned by The Reader's Digest, Pleasantville, N.Y.) dates from 1946. In the spring of 1947 he came down with pneumonia; his friend, the young painter Nicolas de Staël, got him admitted to the American Hospital in Neuilly and there he recovered. These successive bouts of illness weakened his robust constitution, but by no means impaired his faculties; these, on the contrary, now progressively interiorized and spiritualized, prepared him for the great burst of creative activity to come. Now, as in 1916-1917, during his periods of rest and inaction, Braque meditated on his art and on the experience of a lifetime. "With age," he says, "art and life become one." These new meditations, added to the old and interspersed with drawings, went to make up the *Cahier* published in 1948, full of pithy sayings whose wisdom sometimes seems very close—owing to an underlying similarity of outlook, not to any direct influence—to that of Chinese Taoism and Zen Buddhism. With the artificial dividing line blotted out for good, every great modern artist of the past century has gone in quest of a universal humanism in which East und West unite. For Braque the essential thing is to do away with the obfuscating idea or concept ("A picture is finished when it has effaced the idea behind it"), to rediscover the original void antecedent to all creation ("The vase gives form to the void, and music to silence"), and thus to escape from prejudices, conventions,

THE BILLIARD TABLE, 1944. MUSÉE D'ART MODERNE, PARIS.

hindrances, theoretical and emotional mechanisms, and "to keep one's head clear and be present." In this state of perfect open-mindedness, he aims at "seeking out the common, which is not the similar," at maintaining "hope against the ideal, constancy against habit, faith against convictions, the perpetual against the eternal, spirituality against ideality."

Braque was awarded first prize at the 1948 Venice Biennale. That same year he reaffirmed his mastery with a work of almost disconcerting simplicity, *The Chair* (owned by the artist), an

THE CHAIR, 1948. OWNED BY THE ARTIST.

ideogram as pure as Van Gogh's *Chair*, a spare form outlined against a bare luminous wall as succulent and full-bodied as the two pieces of fruit lying on the metal chair. Garden chairs of the same kind appear in the admirable *Terrace* (Dr Hänggi Collection, Vaduz), an intimist, open-air composition.

Braque now, in the late forties, entered what proved to be a climacteric phase of his evolution. The fantastic, convoluted *Billiard Table* of 1949 (Block Collection, Chicago) suddenly became the pole of attraction of unpredictable mirages. Differing from the more solidly constructed *Billiard Tables* of 1944-1945, this freer version has the same visionary élan that fills the *Studio* series, eight vast canvases on which he worked simultaneously, as strange and complex as Uccello's *Battles of San Romano*. The first five were finished in 1949, the three others, interrupted by illness, in 1950-1951, 1954-1955, and 1954-1956 respectively. Each one is numbered. *Studio VII*, begun before Nº VIII but not finished till afterwards, has become Nº IX, now that Nº VII no longer exists.

This key picture sequence, with its esoteric undertones, has been closely and discerningly studied by John Richardson (*The Burlington Magazine* and *L'Oeil*, June 1955), who watched them come into being in the artist's studio and recorded Braque's observations and changes of approach in the course of the work. "I have made a great discovery—I no longer believe in anything," Braque is quoted as saying. "Objects do not exist for me except insofar as a harmonious relationship exists between them and also between them and myself. When one attains to this harmony, one reaches a sort of intellectual non-existence which makes everything possible and right. Life then becomes a perpetual revelation. That is true poetry." The 1947-1955 supplement to the *Cahier*, whose maxims cover precisely the period of the *Studios*, also bears witness to this transfigurative illumination that came over Braque on the threshold of old age:

I am no longer concerned with metaphor, but with metamorphosis.
Forget about things and consider only their interrelationships.
Reality only reveals itself when illuminated by a ray of poetry.

This inspired revelation is embodied in the Protean world of the *Studios*, where objects coexist in perpetual metamorphosis, where space at every turn is reorganized, where the equivocal and ambiguous become vehicles of poetry. Since the 17th century at least, with Rembrandt, Vermeer and Velazquez, the theme of the studio has come to haunt the painters who deal with it, either in literal or in symbolic terms. Matisse and Picasso have repeatedly drawn dazzling or passionate variations from it. Braque has no doubt gone further than any of them in his investigation and transposition of the theme. Summing up the experience of a lifetime and coming as an autobiographical message complete, circumstantial and spiritual in tenor, the *Studios* throw a visionary light on the familiar setting of his daily work and, like *Las Meninas* and the Vienna Vermeer, on the esthetic of a great artist; and on painting itself revealed unawares in all its magic.

When you call on Picasso, he comes out to meet you and bids you welcome with all his overwhelming vitality. It is the man himself, not the artist, who wins you over at once, and painting, or any other art form, is no more to him than a means of liberating the volcanic forces at work within him. His creative powers are always on the ready; any room, wherever he makes his home or stops for the night, will serve him as a studio. His urgent need to communicate tends to surpass his means of communicating, great though they are.

With Braque, whose genius lies in steadiness, in patience and constancy rather than meteoric brilliance, vision and execution coincide absolutely. Painting for him is an end in itself and no existence is possible away from his studio, or rather the two complementary studios which he has had so carefully fitted up in Paris and at Varengeville, and which have been so often described and photographed, with their spacious volume, the subdued light coming in from the south, the concentric arrangement (similar to that of his paintings) of the easels and the objects around the "focus of intensity" formed by the latest picture on the stocks. When you call on Braque, his secretary Mariette Lachaud receives you and shows you in to this wonderful laboratory which holds you spellbound for a moment, until you catch sight of the bright eye, white hair and calm, nobly chiseled features, the beautiful face, of Braque himself, with a smear of the velvet brown of his paintings on his workman's blouse, seated in a corner patiently waiting, the picture of self-effacement before the silent radiance of his work.

Of the eight *Studios*, two—*Studio I* (J.P. Guerlain Collection, Paris) and *Studio V* (Samuel A. Marx Collection, Chicago)—are in Braque's own opinion "special cases" and stand apart, owing either to the simplicity of their treatment or to the partial character of their development. The six others link up to form a visionary cycle of an almost unexampled figurative and rhythmic intricacy. Among the identifiable objects and arbitrary forms poetically mingled in a flexible space of variable density, each of the six versions includes a large bird, variously stylized, which has given rise to much conjecture. It first appeared in a canvas since destroyed. Treated to begin with as a "painting within the painting," the bird subsequently takes wing and flies across the studio, imparting movement and transubstantiation to space. René Char, in a dialogue of the Poet and the Painter, comments on them as follows. "What I like about the picture sequence that you call *The Painter's Studio*, is your having accumulated and heaped up with inspired ingratitude all the eminent yet so very commonplace powers of your reverie and your daily work. They uplift and urge each other on. And this ring-dove, this phoenix rather, now drunk with speed, now

STUDIO III, 1949. DR PAUL HÄNGGI COLLECTION, VADUZ, LIECHTENSTEIN.

rounded off, whether crossing or eying the fleecy sky of your studio, diffuses a breath of wind and a presence that bestir all your recent painting."

Studio II (Niarchos Collection, Paris), replete and compact, and *Studio IV* (Sacher Collection, Basel), less dense, with easel, palette and bird reciprocally magnifying each other, are scored

STUDIO VI, 1950-1951. AIMÉ MAEGHT COLLECTION, PARIS.

with verticals giving the impression of an undulating, palpable surface, like the sheets of cardboard on which Braque carefully lays out his tools. *Studio III* (Dr Hänggi Collection, Vaduz) and *Studio VI* (Maeght Collection, Paris), involved and obscure, evoke a fluid, almost liquid medium, pervious to interchanges, in which objects alternately emerge and dissolve. These four versions are painted on a black ground, in a restrained range of grays, browns and buff, here and there relieved by broken gleams; their grandiose cadence is that of the organ or oratorio. "There was a subdued note in the light of my studio," Braque explains, but, as in the early days of Cubism, this neutral color scheme may also be justified by his concentration on new spatial problems. *Studio VIII* (Private Collection, France), outstanding for its boldness and driving power, one of the artist's major works, and *Studio IX* (Maeght Collection, Paris), built up in the square format which Braque has so brilliantly mastered, are a tissue of luminous colors (deriving from the stained-glass windows he designed in the interval, in 1953-1954, for a country chapel at Varengeville), orchestrating the novel relationships of forms and space.

While perhaps the most impressive, the *Studios* are not the only fruit of this golden autumn. In 1952, a year as productive and diverse as 1942, but in a very different style, before austere and hermetic, now joyful and expansive, Braque recast and successfully finished several large canvases that had been on the stocks for years: a *Reclining Bather* (Maeght Collection, Paris), begun in 1930; a *Billiard Table* (Gelman Collection, Mexico City), begun in 1944, laid out perpendicularly instead of edgewise; and a *Still Life on a Table (Le Grand Guéridon)*, owned by the artist, begun in 1939 and almost Matissian in its sonority. He also worked out some new compositions, often in the open air, brushed in a kind of broadened impressionism: *The Bench* (Irigoyen Collection, Buenos Aires), *The Philodendron* (Phillips Collection, Washington) and *The Bicycle* (Rosensaft Collection, New York), to mention only the most characteristic. The bicycle leans against an easel in the open countryside—a northern countryside of lush green, yellowing under a mauve gray sky, recorded in all its freshness and dilating vitality. The bicycle, that of his youth, on which he used to cycle from Paris to the

THE BICYCLE, 1952. COLLECTION OF MR AND MRS JOSEF ROSENSAFT, NEW YORK.

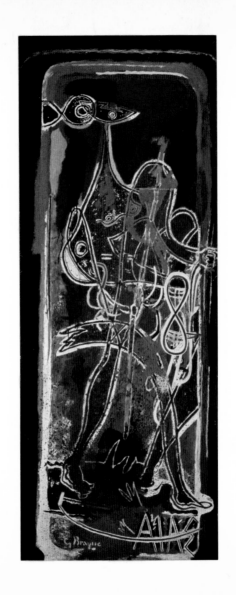

Channel coast, is enclosed in a network both linear and *tachiste*, violet, Naples yellow and khaki-colored, not far removed from the intricacy of the *Studios*; the black bicycle seat is shaped like a bird. Here, as in the *Mantelpieces*, two systems of representation are unforgettably combined. Braque's evolution follows a dual rhythm: simple works "expressing direct emotion" alternate with elaborate compositions in which "the rule corrects emotion." Also in 1952, as a counterpoise to these visionary essays, he painted some flower pieces, sometimes including large vases (G. H. Clouzot Collection, Paris, and Daelemans Collection, Brussels); the truthfulness of these flowers fascinated and disarmed Giacometti: "Gray, brown, black, leaves, sand, vases; the big yellow flowers looking at me... I look at the flowers... How to express the sensation aroused in me by the slightly off-center vertical of the vase and flowers rising up against the gray background?... But why, of all Braque's recent paintings, is it the yellow ochre vase that remains most vivid in my memory? Perhaps because by holding fast and giving so much weight to a single part of the simplest surface, and of what in a sense is the most insignificant of objects, he thereby enhances everything he doesn't paint, he sets a value on what were the dullest and most worthless of things and magnifies all the others that transcend them, and even the spectator himself." This indeed is the painter's mission: to teach us to see by educating our eye, by never regarding any object with indifference or contempt.

In 1951 Braque produced the fabulous composition entitled *Night* (Maeght Collection, Paris) and in 1955, in the neo-classical style of the incised plaster panels, the intrepid silhouette of *Ajax* (Marx Collection, Chicago), a legendary figuration of the hero, warrior and hardened athlete that the artist too must embody, both for himself and the world, if he means to preserve

◄ AJAX, 1955. COLLECTION OF MR AND MRS SAMUEL A. MARX, CHICAGO.

his secret tenderness. But the motif in the true sense of the word, the source of inspiration and movement that was to engross him more and more, was that of the bird. This is the central theme of the ceiling decoration he painted in the Etruscan Gallery of the Louvre (1952-1953), commissioned by Georges Salles, then Director of French Museums; of the decorative panels for the living room of M. Aimé Maeght's villa at Saint-Paul de Vence (1954); and of a number of paintings, lithographs and incised plaster panels. Among the paintings on this theme, *The Bird returning to its Nest* (1956, owned by the artist) was chosen by Braque to represent him in 1958 at the Brussels World's Fair, where its stark splendor stood out radiantly amid a galaxy of masterpieces. A metaphor of the palette with its winged curves, the white migratory bird is seen on its way back to the nest from which it sprang—an anvil-shaped nest painted lifesize. A fervid sense of flight is paradoxically evoked by a sublimated impasto of dark earthy colors.

Braque's birds are not symbolic. Braque is quite explicit on this point: there are no symbols in his painting; meanings are always included in appearances, and poetry in its embodiment. This bird is the organic principle of movement, the *universal* figure of space. "All my life," he recently remarked, "my great concern has been to paint space." And not only to paint it but to make us feel and touch it, to express its palpable essence, its sensuous substance. Cubist space, coexisting with objects, was first of all volumetric and compact, like an embossed bas-relief. Then volume was opened up, broken up into facets, aligned along the picture plane in echeloned thinnesses, until the limit was reached with *papiers collés*. Thereafter space was tackled frontally, and we have followed the progressive solution of the problem in tactile terms—palms outstretched toward the walls that recede under the pressure of objects, of curved masses against angular masses, finally defining the entire room space

THE BIRD RETURNING TO ITS NEST, 1956. OWNED BY THE ARTIST.

contained within four walls, including on occasion an open window—quadrangular, "cubic" space inhabited by man and his tutelary objects, space measurable, with the greatest accuracy, in terms of man, of feet and inches. With the *Studios* the organization of forms, structure and texture is modified; delivered from proprieties and uses, objects acquire "a new destiny" and lend themselves to metamorphoses; ceasing to be architectural and figurable in the cubist idiom, space becomes undulating, fluctuating, dynamic and sidereal, eludes human measure and belongs only to birds.

Suspended between sky and earth, with its roots in space and its home in the clouds, the bird, unattached link of nature's elements, lives and has its being in a new element—movement. This is the *bird of matter* (René de Solier) in a *space before ideas* (Jean Paulhan). For the elasticity of space and the movement of flight imply the density of matter. In the ceiling decoration of the Louvre, so simple and grandiose, governed by the birds wheeling above an Etruscan sarcophagus, the dark blue of the sky is as thick as tar.

"The true materialist," says Braque, "is the believer." And matter for him is the source and mainstay of spirituality; matter is "what stirs the sense of touch." The universality of space reposes on the community of matter, on its *humility*. It is the primeval humus, the diluvial *limus* of Creation, the gray and brown substance that has always formed the principal sediment of Braque's painting. Of his recent pictures in particular, with their thick and miry impasto shot with muffled gleams, of which the time has not yet come to speak, for the cycle is still unfolding. Along with the bird, they represent the cosmic field of his evolution, the plain, the sea, the sky, in the breath of daytime and, more and more often, in the deeper breath of night. With matter in his grasp, that mysterious, thickly spread substance which is the body of his painting and the soul of the universe, Braque molds space in his workman's hands and renders the infinite tangible.

SELECTED BIBLIOGRAPHY
EXHIBITIONS
INDEX OF NAMES AND PLACES
LIST OF COLORPLATES
CONTENTS

SELECTED BIBLIOGRAPHY

General

A. GLEIZES and J. METZINGER, *Du Cubisme*, Paris 1912; in English, London 1913. — G. APOLLINAIRE, *Les Peintres cubistes*, Paris 1913; in English, New York 1949. — A. SALMON, *L'Art vivant*, Paris 1920. — D. HENRY (D. H. Kahnweiler), *Der Weg zum Kubismus*, Munich 1920; American ed., *The Rise of Cubism*, New York 1949. — Carl EINSTEIN, *Die Kunst des 20. Jahrhunderts*, Berlin 1926 and 1931. — M. RAYNAL, *Anthologie de la Peinture française*, Paris 1927. — A. BRETON, *Le Surréalisme et la peinture*, Paris 1928. — G. JANNEAU, *L'Art cubiste*, Paris 1929. — F. OLIVIER, *Picasso et ses amis*, Paris 1933. — R. HUYGHE, *Histoire de l'Art contemporain*, Paris 1935. — A. BARR, *Cubism and Abstract Art*, New York 1936. — C. ZERVOS, *Histoire de l'Art contemporain*, Paris 1938. — G. DUTHUIT, *Les Fauves*, Geneva 1949; in English, New York 1950. — M. RAYNAL and others, *History of Modern Painting*, Vol. III: *From Picasso to Surrealism*, Geneva 1950. — P. FRANCASTEL, *Peinture et Société*, Lyon 1951. — C. STERLING, *La Nature morte de l'Antiquité à nos jours*, Paris 1952 and 1959; in English, New York 1959. — W. HAFTMANN, *Malerei im 20. Jahrhundert*, Munich 1954-1955. — P. HERON, *The Changing Forms of Art*, London 1955. — G. SCHMIDT, *Petite histoire de la Peinture moderne*, Neuchâtel 1956. — B. DORIVAL, *Peintres du XXe siècle*, Paris 1957; in English, New York 1958. — G. HABASQUE, *Cubism*, Geneva 1959. — J. LEYMARIE, *Fauvism*, Geneva 1959. — J. GOLDING, *Cubism*, London 1959. — J. GRENIER, *Essais sur la Peinture contemporaine*, Paris 1959. — J. CASSOU, *Panorama des arts plastiques contemporains*, Paris 1960.

Writings and Statements by the Artist

Pensées et Réflexions sur la Peinture, in *Nord-Sud*, December 1917. — *Cahier de Georges Braque*: 1917-1947, Paris 1948; with supplement 1947-1955, Paris 1956. Cheap edition published as: *Le Jour et la Nuit*, 1917-1952, Paris 1952. — *Réponses à une enquête*, in *Cahiers d'Art*, No. 10, 1935; *Cahiers d'Art*, No. 14, 1939; *Les Lettres Françaises*, March 15, 1946. — Statements recorded by G. Jedlicka, *Begegnung mit Georges Braque*, in *Begegnungen*, Basel 1933; by Gaston Diehl, *L'Univers pictural et son Destin, une conversation avec Georges Braque*, in *Les Problèmes de la Peinture*, Paris 1945; by E. Tériade, in *Verve*, 1952, vol. VII, No. 27-28; by A. Imaizumi, in the Japanese review *Misue*, October 1952; by Georges Ribemont-Dessaignes, in *Arts*, September 1953; by Dora Vallier, *Braque, la peinture et nous*, in *Cahiers d'Art*, No. 1, 1954 (essential); by John Richardson, in *The Observer*, December 1, 1957 (important); by Georges Charbonnier, in *Le monologue du peintre*, Paris 1959.

Catalogues

A complete catalogue of Braque's work is being prepared by the Galerie Maeght, Paris; two volumes have now been published, edited by N. Mangin: *Peintures 1948-1957*, Paris 1959, and *Peintures 1942-1947*, Paris 1960. — A tentative catalogue for the period 1906-1929 was published by George Isarlo, *Georges Braque*, Paris 1932. — Catalogue raisonné of the graphic work by R. Engelberts, Geneva 1958.

Monographs

R. BISSIÈRE, *Georges Braque*, Paris 1920. — M. RAYNAL, *Georges Braque*, Rome 1924. — G. ISARLO, *Georges Braque*, Paris 1932. — Carl EINSTEIN, *Georges Braque*, Paris 1934. — Stanislas FUMET, *Braque*, Paris 1941 and 1945. — A. E. GALLATIN, *Georges Braque*, New York 1943. — J. PAULHAN, *Braque le Patron*, Paris 1945 and 1952; Geneva 1946. — F. PONGE, *Braque le Réconciliateur*, Geneva 1947. — J. GRENIER, *Braque: Peintures 1942-1947*, Paris 1948. — D. COOPER, *Braque: Paintings 1909-1947*, London 1948. — P. REVERDY, *Une aventure méthodique*, Paris 1949. — H. R. HOPE, *Georges Braque*, New York 1949. — A. LEJARD, *Braque*, Paris 1949. — F. PONGE, *Braque, Dessins*, Paris 1950. — Stanislas FUMET, *Sculptures de Georges Braque*, Paris 1951. — L. G. BUCHHEIM, *Georges Braque, Das graphische Werk*, Feldafing 1952. — M. SEUPHOR, *L'œuvre graphique de Braque*, Paris 1953. — F. LAUFER, *Georges Braque*, Bern 1954. — J. CASSOU, *Braque*, Paris 1956. — M. GIEURE, *Georges Braque*, Paris 1956; in English, New York 1958. — *Braque*, Geneva 1956. — P. HERON, *Braque*, London (n.d.). — A. VERDET, M. GIEURE, *Georges Braque: Dessins*, Paris 1956. — A. VERDET, *Georges Braque le solitaire*, Paris 1959. — J. RICHARDSON, *Georges Braque*, London 1959. — J. RUSSELL, *Georges Braque*, London 1959. — J. RICHARDSON, *Georges Braque*, Milan 1960. — Christian ZERVOS, *Georges Braque, Nouvelles Sculptures et Plaques gravées*, Paris 1960.

Special Numbers of Periodicals

Les Soirées de Paris, April 15, 1914. — *Cahiers d'Art*, 1933, No. 1/2 (texts by R. Bissière, A. Breton, J. Cassou, B. Cendrars, H. E. Ede, Carl Einstein, A. Lhote, A. Salmon, A. Soffici, C. Zervos). — *Misue*, Tokyo, October 1952 (texts by A. Imaizumi and F. Ponge). — *Le Point*, Souillac, October 1953 (texts by Stanislas Fumet, G. Limbour, G. Ribemont-Dessaignes). — *Verve*, 1955, Vol. VIII, No. 31/32, *Les Carnets intimes de Georges Braque* (texts by Will Grohmann, A. Tudal, R. West). — *Derrière le Miroir*, June 1947 (texts by René Char and J. Kober). — *Derrière le Miroir*, January 1950 (texts by R. Char, A. Maldiney, J. Guignard). — *Derrière le Miroir*, June-July 1952 (texts by A. Giacometti, J. Grenier). — *Derrière le Miroir*, October-November 1954 (text by G. Limbour). — *Derrière le Miroir*, April-May 1956 (text by J. Dupin). — *Derrière le Miroir*, 1959 (text by G. Charbonnier).

Magazine Articles

L. Vauxcelles, *Gil Blas*, March 10 and November 14, 1908; March 25, 1909. — G. Apollinaire, *Le Mercure de France*, January 16, 1909. — A. Soffici, *Picasso e Braque*, in *La Voce*, Florence, August 24, 1911. — A. Lhote, *Nouvelle Revue Française*, June 1, 1919. — W. George, *Georges Braque*, in *L'Esprit Nouveau*, 1, 1921. — H. Hertz, *Braque et le réveil des apparences*, in *L'Amour de l'Art*, Paris 1926. — E. Tériade, *Les dessins de Georges Braque*, in *Cahiers d'Art*, 11, 1927. — C. Zervos, *Georges Braque et la peinture française*, in *Cahiers d'Art*, 11, 1927. — E. Tériade, *L'épanouissement de l'œuvre de Braque*, in *Cahiers d'Art*, 1, 1928. — J. Cassou, *Georges Braque*, in *Cahiers d'Art*, 1, 1928. — Carl Einstein, *Tableaux récents de Georges Braque*, in *Documents*, 1929. — Will Grohmann, *Georges Braque*, in *Cicerone*, 1929. — C. Zervos, *Observations sur les peintures récentes de Georges Braque*, in *Cahiers d'Art*, v, 1930. — R. Cogniat, *Braque et les Ballets Russes*, in *L'Amour de l'Art*, May 1931. — C. Zervos, *Le classicisme de Braque*, in *Cahiers d'Art*, vi, 1931. — C. Zervos, *Georges Braque et le développement du Cubisme*, in *Cahiers d'Art*, 1-2, 1932. — A. Lhote, *Le symbolisme plastique de Georges Braque*, in *Nouvelle Revue Française*, No. 48, 1937. — C. Zervos, *Braque et la Grèce primitive*, in *Cahiers d'Art*, No. 22, 1940. — J. Paulhan, *Braque ou le sens du caché*, in *Cahiers d'Art*, 1940-1944. — J. Babelon, *Braque et la nature morte*, in *Beaux-Arts*, September 30, 1943. — G. Bazin, *Braque*, in *Labyrinthe*, January 15, 1945. — J. Ambler, *The Gallic Traditionalism of Braque*, in *Bulletin of the City Art Museum*, St. Louis, April 1945. — J. Cassou, *Le secret de Braque*, in *L'Amour de l'Art*, January 1946. — A. Jakowski, *Georges Braque*, in *Arts de France*, viii, 1946. — J. Grenier, *Introduction à la peinture de Georges Braque*, in *Variété*, No. 3, 1946. — F. Ponge, *Braque le Réconciliateur*, in *Labyrinthe*, December 23, 1946. — C. Zervos, *Œuvres de Braque*, in *Cahiers d'Art*, No. 22, 1947. — G. Rosenthal, *The Art of Braque*, Baltimore Museum of Art, *Museum News*, April 1948. — A. M. Frankfurter, *Georges Braque*, in *Art News*, February 1949. — M. Arland, *Braque*, in *L'Age Nouveau*, No. 42, 1949. — L. Degand, *Braque*, in *Art d'Aujourd'hui*, No. 7-8, 1950. — J. Bouret, *Braque ou l'andante noir et gris*, in *Arts*, February 17, 1950. — C. Zervos, *Georges Braque*, in *Cahiers d'Art*, No. 25, 1950. — R. Char, *Georges Braque*, in *Cahiers d'Art*, No. 26, 1951. — R. de Solier, *L'œuvre gravé de Braque*, in *Cahiers de la Pléiade*, xii, 1951. — G. Bazin, *Sur l'espace en peinture: la vision de Braque*, in *Journal de Psychologie*, No. 45, 1953. — G. Jedlicka, *Georges Braque*, in *Universitas*, Stuttgart, ix, 1954. — J. Richardson, *The Ateliers of Braque*, in *The Burlington Magazine*, June 1955. — J. Richardson, *Le nouvel Atelier de Braque*, in *L'Œil*, June 1955. — M. Vincent, *Un tableau de Braque*, in *Bulletin des Musées lyonnais*, iv, 1955. — L. Gowing, *Two Contemporaries, Braque and Ben Nicholson*, in *New Statesman*, April 1957. — G. Limbour, *Georges Braque, Découvertes et traditions*, in *L'Œil*, September 1957. — R. de Solier, *L'Oiseau de Braque*, in *Cahiers d'Art*, No. 31-32, 1956-1957. —

J. Leymarie, *Georges Braque, L'Oiseau et son nid*, in *Quadrum*, v, 1958. — J. E. Clemente, *Braque pintor del Soledad*, in *La Nación*, Buenos Aires, August 31, 1958. — P. Francastel, *Braque e il Cubismo*, in *La Biennale di Venezia*, August 1958. — C. Greenberg, *Pasted Papers Revolution*, in *Art News*, September 1958. — J. Selz, *L'Oiseau et la Grève*, in *Lettres Nouvelles*, July 1959.

EXHIBITIONS

1908, November 9-28, Paris, Galerie Kahnweiler (catalogue with preface by Guillaume Apollinaire). — 1919, March 5-31, Paris, Galerie Léonce Rosenberg. — 1922, Paris, Salon d'Automne. — 1924, May 2-21, Paris, Galerie Paul Rosenberg. — 1925, March, Berlin, Galerie Flechtheim. — 1926, March 8-24, Galerie Paul Rosenberg. — 1930, May, Paris, Galerie Paul Rosenberg. — 1933, April 9-May 14, Basel, Kunsthalle (catalogue with introduction by Carl Einstein). — 1934, July, London, Alex Reid and Lefèvre Galleries. — 1936, January 8-31, Paris, Galerie Paul Rosenberg. — 1936, July, London, Alex Reid and Lefèvre Galleries. — 1936, November, Brussels, Palais des Beaux-Arts. — 1937, April 3-30, Paris, Galerie Paul Rosenberg. — 1938, February 4-21, Paris, Galerie Pierre (Fauve period). — 1938, July, London, Paul Rosenberg and Helft Ltd. — 1938, October 14-25, New York, Buchholz Gallery. — 1938, November 16-December 10, Paris, Galerie Paul Rosenberg. — 1939, April 4-29, Paris, Galerie Paul Rosenberg. — 1939, November 7-29, Arts Club of Chicago (catalogue with preface by Henry McBride and introduction by J. J. Sweeney). — 1939-1940, December 6-January 6, Washington, Duncan Phillips Memorial Gallery (catalogue with texts by Duncan Phillips, Henry McBride and J. J. Sweeney). — 1943, September 25-October 31, Paris, Salon d'Automne. — 1945, October 20-November 12, Amsterdam, Stedelijk Museum. — 1945, November 24-December 13, Brussels, Palais de Beaux-Arts. — 1946, May, London, Tate Gallery, *Braque and Rouault*, (catalogue with introduction by Germain Bazin). — 1947, June, Paris, Galerie Maeght. — 1948, January 5-24, New York, Paul Rosenberg Gallery. — 1948, May-October, Venice Biennale. — 1948, September, Geneva, Athénée. — 1949, New York, Museum of Modern Art, and Cleveland Museum of Art (catalogue with introduction by Jean Cassou, texts by H. R. Hope and W. S. Lieberman). — 1950, September, Stockholm, Samlaren Gallery. — 1952, June-July, Paris, Galerie Maeght. — 1952, August, Tokyo, Yomiuri. — 1952, October 6-25, New York, Paul Rosenberg Gallery. — 1953, April 25-May 31, Bern, Kunsthalle (catalogue with preface by Arnold Rüdlinger). — 1953, June-July, Zurich, Kunsthaus. — 1953, November 14-December 6, Liège, Musée des Beaux-Arts, *L'œuvre graphique* (catalogue with preface by Michel Seuphor).— 1954, May 14-July 3, London, Institute of Contemporary Arts (paintings and drawings from English private collections). — 1955, January-July, Cologne,

Bremen, Düsseldorf, Krefeld, Berlin, *Das graphische Gesamtwerk 1907-1955* (catalogue with preface by P. Wember). — 1956, May-June, Paris, Galerie Maeght. — 1956-1957, December-January, Cincinnati Art Museum, *The Sculpture of Georges Braque* (catalogue with preface by Jean Leymarie). — 1956, Edinburgh, The Royal Scottish Academy, and London, Tate Gallery (catalogue and introduction by Douglas Cooper). — 1958, Rome, Palazzo Barberini (presentation by R. Pallucchini). — 1958, Venice Biennale (preface by Jacques Lassaigne). — 1958, Geneva, Galerie Rauch, *L'œuvre graphique originale* (catalogue with poems by René Char and text by E. Engelberts). — 1958, Paris, Galerie Maeght, *Grands livres illustrés* (catalogue with a poem by A. Tudal and text by R. Vieillard). — 1959, Paris, Galerie Maeght. — 1960, April 9-May 29, Basel, Kunsthalle (catalogue with preface by Arnold Rüdlinger and introduction by Pierre Volboudt). — 1960, Paris, Bibliothèque Nationale, *L'œuvre graphique* (catalogue by J. Adhémar and J. Lethève, with introductions by J. Cain and J. Valléry-Radot).

INDEX OF NAMES AND PLACES

Havre Le 5, 6, 13/15, 20; Ecole des Beaux-Arts 5, 14, 20; Lycée 5, 14, 20; Musée des Beaux-Arts 6, 16.
HEGEL Georg Wilhelm Friedrich (1770-1831) 70.
Hellenistic painting 29.
HENRAUX Albert 15.
HILDEBRAND Adolf von (1847-1921) 46.
Honfleur 6, 13, 16.
Horta de San Juan (near Tarragona) 6, 41.

Iberian sculpture 29.
Ile-de-France 101.
Impressionism and its influence 13, 20/22, 25, 27, 32, 38, 46, 56; The Impressionists 13, 16, 31, 32.
INGRES Jean-Dominique (1780-1867) 15.

JACOB Max (1876-1944) 7, 59.
JOUVET Louis (1887-1951) 9.
JOYCE James (1882-1941) 44.
Juan-les-Pins 76.

KAHNWEILER Daniel-Henry 6, 28, 32; Collection 53, 56; Gallery, Braque Exhibition (1908) 6, 35, 36; Simon Gallery 7.

LABERTHE 14.
LACHAUD Mariette, Braque's secretary 107.
LAPRÉ Marcelle, Braque's wife 7.
LAURENCIN Marie (1885-1956) 5, 16.
LAURENS Henri (1885-1954) 7, 62, 97.
LAUTREC Henri de Toulouse- (1864-1901) 5, 14.
LÉGER Fernand (1881-1955) 9, 38.
Limousin 8, 93.
London, Sir Antony Hornby Collection 45, 48; Roland, Browse & Delbanco Collection 102;

Tate Gallery, Braque Exhibition (1946, with Rouault) 9; (1956) 9; Reid & Lefèvre Galleries, Braque Exhibition (1934) 8.
Loos Adolf (1870-1933), architect 44.

MAEGHT Aimé, picture dealer 114; Braque Exhibition (1947) 9.
MANET Edouard (1832-1883) 11, 16, 36, 48, 52.
MANOLO, sculptor 6.
MARQUET Albert (1875-1947) 9, 19, 21, 35.
Mantes 6, 40.
Marseilles 6, 22, 24, 56.
Martigues, Les 33.
MATISSE Henri (1869-1954) 6, 9, 19, 21, 22, 24, 27, 31, 35, 36, 63, 80, 87, 97, 101, 106, 110.
Mediterranean 40, 81.
Mercure de France (1907) 28.
Meriden (Conn.), Mrs Burton Tremaine Collection 76.
Mexico City, Gelman Collection 110.
MONET Claude (1840-1926) 13, 16.
MOREAU Gustave 19.
MOURLOT, printer (Paris) 9.
MOZART Wolfgang Amadeus (1756-1791) 71.

Negro sculpture 29, 35.
Neuilly, American Hospital 102.
New York, Museum of Modern Art 31, 49, 51, 52, 77, 87, 88, 90; Braque Exhibition (1948/49) 9; Armory Show (Exhibition) (1913) 7; Solomon R. Guggenheim Museum 42, 43, 48; Collections: Samuel A. Berger 22; Walter P. Chrysler Jr. 34, 40, 49, 84, 89, 91; Mr and Mrs Werner E. Josten 23, 25, 28; Mrs Albert D. Lasker 83,

LIST OF COLORPLATES

133

CONTENTS

THIS, THE THIRTY-FIFTH VOLUME OF "THE TASTE OF OUR TIME"
SERIES, WAS PRODUCED BY THE TECHNICAL STAFF OF
EDITIONS D'ART ALBERT SKIRA, FINISHED THE TWENTY-FIFTH
DAY OF FEBRUARY NINETEEN HUNDRED AND SIXTY-ONE.

TEXT AND ILLUSTRATIONS BY

COLOR STUDIOS
AT IMPRIMERIES RÉUNIES S.A., LAUSANNE.

PLATES ENGRAVED BY GUEZELLE AND RENOUARD, PARIS.

PHOTOGRAPHS BY

*Henry B. Beville, Washington (pages 17, 23, 34, 42, 43, 46, 51, 64, 65, 68, 69, 70,
72, 73, 82, 83, 84, 86, 88, 89, 90, 111, 112 and the back of the jacket), Sven Nilsson,
Stockholm (page 36), Zoltan Wegner, London (pages 19, 45), Louis Laniepce,
Paris (pages 53, 55, 74, 78, 104, 109, 115), Charles Uht, New York (page 59),
Hans Hinz, Basel (pages 61 96, 108), and F. W. Sliders, Houston (page 98).*

PRINTED IN SWITZERLAND